NATIVE
PERENNIALS

NORTH AMERICAN BEAUTIES

Nancy Beaubaire, Guest Editor

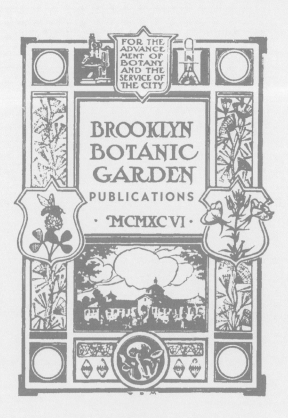

Janet Marinelli
SERIES EDITOR

Beth Hanson
ASSOCIATE EDITOR

Bekka Lindstrom
ART DIRECTOR

Stephen K.M. Tim
VICE PRESIDENT, SCIENCE, LIBRARY & PUBLICATIONS

Judith D. Zuk
PRESIDENT

Elizabeth Scholtz
DIRECTOR EMERITUS

Handbook #146

Copyright © Spring 1996 by the Brooklyn Botanic Garden, Inc.

BBG gardening books are published quarterly at 1000 Washington Ave., Brooklyn, NY 11225

Subscription included in Brooklyn Botanic Garden membership dues ($35.00 per year)

ISSN # 0362-5850 ISBN # 0-945352-92-1

Printed by Science Press, a division of the Mack Printing Group

Table of Contents

ENCYCLOPEDIA OF NATIVE PERENNIALS

Garden-worthy Native Perennials

BY NANCY BEAUBAIRE

I WAS FIRST SMITTEN by native plants in the early seventies in California. I came to these plants not as a gardener, although I was one, but to satisfy an irrepressible urge to learn about how the indigenous people of the West used the plants around them. I devoured every book I could on the subject, committing to memory the visual characteristics of each plant so I would recognize it in the flesh. I hiked along the beach and through redwood forests, wended my way through chaparral and scrambled up mountains, always on the lookout for native plants. Sometimes I hiked alone, other times with the California Native Plant Society, but always accompanied by my faithful (and weighty) local guidebooks.

Wild ginger (*Asarum caudatum*) was one of my first discoveries. Stumbling upon a carpet of its heart-shaped leaves nestled in the shade of a giant redwood tree was a transcendental moment for me. Here was a plant whose aromatic root yielded a ginger flavor, and whose handsome dark green leaves rivaled any patch of periwinkle.

Similar experiences followed with other native perennials. Penstemon, cardinal flower, yarrow and Douglas iris all captured my heart. I'd like to say that from those moments on, I began incorporating native perennials into my own gardens and those I designed for others. But I didn't.

Despite my deep appreciation of natives, it took a while for me to realize that it was okay to bring them across the line from nature into the garden. The boundary seemed very real, and at that time native plants had few press agents. (An exception and an inspiration to me was landscape designer and teacher

David Bigham, who helped demystify the nitty gritty of growing native plants in a cultivated garden.) More importantly, native perennials were scarcely available commercially. When I finally decided to take the plunge, I trekked 200 miles to get a decent selection, to Yerba Buena Nursery, in Woodside, California, where owner Gerda Isenberg pioneered the propagation of California native plants.

My clients didn't further the cause, either. Nearly all of them were California transplants who brought with them an unwavering desire to surround themselves with the plants they grew up with, many of

Native perennials not only offer interesting foliage and sometimes sizzling colors, but many also make superb cut bouquets.

these water hogs that were ill suited to our rainfall cycle. A long dry spell finally convinced my clients to take a second look at the native perennials that have adapted over thousands of years to the vagaries of the California climate; their good garden qualities won them a permanent home.

Which brings me to the focus of this handbook—garden-worthy native perennials. You may not come to native perennials because of an abiding interest in indigenous people's use of plants. Or because of a drought. Or because of any deep-seated ecological views. But if you're interested in trying some exceptional garden perennials, get out your trowel. Native perennials offer a wealth of flower color, from the sizzling to the subdued, as well as interesting foliage textures and colors. Some even make superb cut bouquets. Some natives form mounds, oth-

You don't need a wild garden to grow native perennials.

ers creep along the ground and still others soar skyward. You don't need a wild garden to grow native perennials. Like non-natives, they can play a variety of roles in your garden—as specimens, in perennial borders or mixed with shrubs or annuals. Planted in the right site, and given proper (and, often, minimal) care, they prosper and bring years of pleasure.

There's more. Growing perennials native to your area can help to repair the fabric of local plant and animal life that has been tattered by decades of intensive development. And in cultivated settings, native perennials begin to create a regional imprint. Your garden will say something about the character of the place where you live, rather than shout "Anywhere, U.S.A."

But no matter why you decide to try native perennials, you can use this handbook as a guide. An easy way to start is to find your floristic province on the map at right. Each province is an area of land where distinctive kinds of plants live together, forming particular vegetation types. While these provinces provide a convenient way to divide up the country, each includes a great diversity of habitats and plant communities. The floristic provinces map can tell you which plants are native to your area; then select species that are suited to your own backyard.

Next, check the "Encyclopedia of Native Perennials" (page 29) for recommended native plants for your region. You might be surprised to find that some of the perennials you already grow, such as columbines, asters, black-eyed Susans, salvias and sunflowers, are in fact native to your floristic province. In the entry for each native perennial, look under the headings "Native Habitat" and "How to Grow" for information on the plant's needs. Each plant entry also includes cultivars and related species, which may have special qualities that better suit your needs than the main entry.

If you have an urge to stretch the limits (and it seems most gardeners do), read about the plants recommended for other regions. You might find some that will

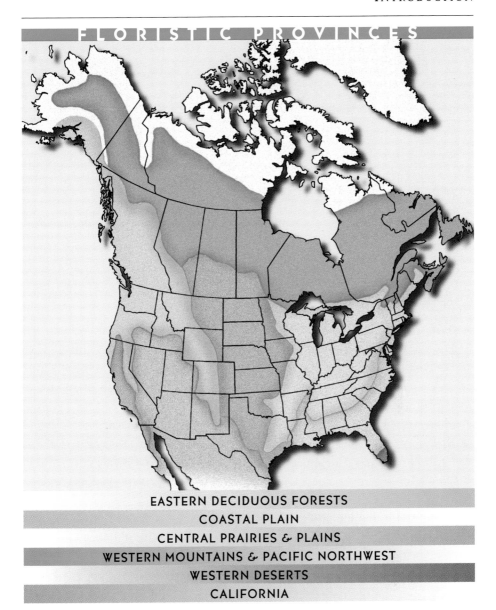

FLORISTIC PROVINCES

EASTERN DECIDUOUS FORESTS
COASTAL PLAIN
CENTRAL PRAIRIES & PLAINS
WESTERN MOUNTAINS & PACIFIC NORTHWEST
WESTERN DESERTS
CALIFORNIA

thrive in your area. Many native perennials have a wide range of adaptability, and may do well in garden conditions that differ from those of their natural habitats.

The chapters "Choosing Native Perennials for Your Garden" (page 8) and "Designing Your Garden with Native Perennials" (page 14) will help you explore the options for incorporating native perennials in your garden. Whatever approach you take, let nature inspire you, experiment and have fun.

Choosing Native Perennials for Your Garden

BY SALLY ROTH

NATIVE PLANTS can create a strong sense of place. Cacti and succulents speak of the desert. Hepatica and Dutchman's breeches evoke springtime under the hardwoods. Spiky pink gayfeathers and radiant sunflowers are the soul of the prairie; icy-white avalanche lilies, of the mountain meadow.

Despite all the evocative qualities of these plants, defining "native" is not only a matter of location; it is also a matter of time. A native plant is one that was indigenous to a particular ecological region about 150 to 200 years ago—before plants were massively displaced or introduced by Europeans.

This book uses ecologically distinct areas called floristic provinces to suggest which native plants will thrive for you. If a plant is native to the desert of southern California, for example, chances are it will also perform well in gardens throughout the floristic province known as the western deserts.

Some ecologically minded gardeners choose to limit their plant choices to only those species indigenous to their region. Some gardeners use regionally native plants for the parts of their property where they're trying to re-create natural habitat, and use plants native to other regions of North America and other continents in their perennial borders and traditional plantings (see "Designing Your Garden with Native Perennials," page 14). Plants from other continents and regions are technically not natives, but they may still be garden-worthy plants. It's up to you to decide which plants to include in your gardens, and how to use them.

Native plants can create a strong sense of place. Pink plains penstemon, left, speaks of the arid West, while Virginia bluebells evoke springtime in the eastern forests.

FLORISTIC PROVINCES

If you don't already have a feel for what plants are native to your area, start by taking a look at the map on page 7. North America is divided into a number of ecologically distinct regions, the floristic provinces. The climate, geology and other conditions throughout a floristic province are similar enough that plants native to one part of a province will generally be adapted to conditions in most other parts. This doesn't mean that all plants native to Ohio, for instance, will also thrive in, say, Tennessee—both states that fall within the boundaries of the floristic province known as the eastern deciduous forests. But many of them will.

This is a simplified system, of course. Within each floristic province there are many smaller, more specialized plant communities. In the eastern deciduous forest province, to continue the example, you'll find not only forests but also marshes, meadows, rocky outcrops—you get the idea. A garden there might have plantings modeled after several of these habitats, each with its associated native species.

As a general rule, floristic provinces are a great tool for getting a quick fix on what plants will work best for you. But keep in mind that unless you're trying to

Within each floristic province there are many smaller, more specialized plant communities. Both bee balms pictured above are native to the eastern states. *Monarda didyma*, right, prefers rich, moist soils; *M. fistulosa* tolerates poorer, drier soils.

re-create native plant communities in your yard, floristic province isn't the last word. Many native plants are adaptable to a much wider area than where they're found growing wild. Fringecups and some other natives of the Pacific Northwest will do nicely in an eastern woodland garden. Maximilian sunflowers and other prairie denizens can be planted in a garden thousands of miles away from the Midwest and won't miss a beat.

THE ALTERED LANDSCAPE

Why is it so difficult to figure out what's native where? Because we humans have long been busily rearranging the planet's flora. We chopped down the immense hardwood forests that once covered much of the eastern half of the country, and replaced the deep sod created by thousands of years of prairie grass in the Midwest with corn and soybeans. Today, a new suburb in Kansas is apt to look just like one in Pennsylvania, which looks just like one in Washington.

Wagon trains and railroads and now interstates and airplanes have accelerated the spread of plants in the wild as well as in cultivation. Eurasian species such as oxeye daisy and Queen Anne's lace have colonized North America with all the fervor of us humans. And so a perennial wildflower in America today is not necessarily a native perennial. (Some of our natives have returned the favor. Hikers and dog owners in Europe are no fonder of our beggar's-ticks than we are of their burdock.)

A small percentage of these introduced plants have become extremely aggressive and invasive, displacing native plants and causing great ecological damage. Dozens of American native grasses and other plants have also become undesirables because of their invasiveness, and some native perennials can also become ecological thugs. Marsh marigold, for example, will rapidly move downstream as storm water sweeps the bulbs onward, colonizing the

Many natives, such as Maximilian sunflower, a prairie denizen, can be planted thousands of miles away from their wild habitat and won't miss a beat.

creek bank as it goes. If you're considering a plant known to be invasive, think twice before introducing it to your neighborhood. A quick phone call to a local preserve or your state branch of the Nature Conservancy will tell you whether your plant is *flora non grata*. When it comes to invasives, prevention is always easier than cure. Some gardeners choose to grow only non-invasive native plants because they know that they won't be introducing a problem species to their area.

LOOKING AT PARTICULARS

Floristic provinces are areas where climate and other conditions are generally similar. But as any good gardener knows, general conditions can vary considerably in their particulars, even from one garden to the next. A river can moderate the climate; a mountain can deny rainwater; a building can create shade or change wind patterns. Even a thirsty tree in the next-door neighbor's yard can make enough of a difference to affect the plants you grow.

Choose native perennials for your site just as you would any other garden plants. If you live in the eastern half of the country, use the USDA hardiness zones as a first step in determining whether a plant will survive in your area (to find your zone, check the map on page 104); if you live in the West, consult the Sunset zones. The USDA and Sunset zones are included in every plant entry in the "Encyclopedia of Native Perennials," beginning on page 29. These zones are a good starting point, but a slew of other factors also affect a plant's performance. For example, it may not be cold winters that restrict the growing area, but rather humid summers, or lack of snow cover, or desiccating wind. Consider the texture and fertility of your soil and its pH. Think about the amount and pattern of rainfall—some natives thrive in bone-dry summers; others require year-round water. Take a look at the light levels in your garden, the number of hours per day of sun or the lack of it. Keep in mind your local temperature patterns. Are there late spring frosts or swings from one extreme to another? To play it safe, choose native perennials that are compatible with what your garden offers.

Of course, many gardeners don't play it safe. We experiment, test a plant's limits—and sometimes this works. If you fall in love with a plant but aren't sure how it will do in your garden, take a chance. Sometimes plant requirements are based only on what's known *so far.* Many native plants show surprising adaptability, flourishing in garden conditions that are very different from those in their natural habitats. Experimenting is part of the fun.

ENHANCING NATURE

We all want our gardens to be like Nature at her most glorious: an alpine meadow or a spring woodland bursting into bloom. We forget that those knock-your-socks-off displays are often fleeting—a couple of weeks after snowmelt or winter rains, a few short weeks before the canopy leafs out, then they're gone. That's where gardening offers advantages. We can plant for maximum effect. By choosing native plants as carefully as other perennials, we can plan for season-long beauty.

When choosing plants, use your common sense and your aesthetic sensibility. You wouldn't stick a saguaro in the middle of a mixed perennial border. But a western penstemon would be right at home. Gardening with natives gives you a heightened sense of what's appropriate. When you combine plants that grow together naturally in the wild, your garden has an instinctive appeal.

When you get down to actually selecting among the candidates for your garden, you'll notice that many popular garden plants are cultivars (short for "cultivated varieties"). A cultivar is a plant with one or more unique characteristics that distinguish it from other members of the same species. Over the years, plants with extra-large flowers or other unusual traits have been pulled out of the

Iris cristata and *Aquilegia canadensis* are both natives of eastern and central states. Some gardeners choose to grow only non-invasive plants indigenous to their area because they know they won't be introducing a problem species.

crowd, named as cultivars, and sent on to fame in the garden world. Hybridists tinkering with various plant crosses have also created their share of cultivars. A cultivar is identified by a name in single quotation marks after the the two-part Latin name that identifies the species: *Rudbeckia fulgida* 'Goldsturm', for example, is a cultivar of the species *Rudbeckia fulgida*. It's more floriferous and a more compact plant than the species.

Typically, cultivars are propagated asexually, usually from cuttings of the parent plant (not sexually, from seed), as that's the only way to preserve the traits for which they've been singled out. So, when you buy *Rudbeckia fulgida* 'Goldsturm' you're buying a clone—a plant that is genetically identical to every other specimen of 'Goldsturm' in existence. Some gardeners prefer to grow only species plants propagated from seed because they do more to promote biodiversity than named cultivars do. Species plants may also be preferred for their "true to nature" look. The double-flowered cultivar of bloodroot ('Multiplex' or 'Flore Pleno'), for example, is certainly a beauty, but its fluffy, extra-large flower doesn't look much like the simple starry blossom of a typical bloodroot. Whether or not a cultivar is necessary for the particular effect you're trying to achieve in your garden is something you'll have to decide for yourself.

Designing Your Garden with Native Perennials

BY KEN DRUSE

PERENNIALS ARE WELCOME in all parts of the garden. They're most often used in herbaceous beds and borders, but they can also be mixed with woody shrubs to create exciting, long-blooming plantings. Perennial gardens can bask in the shade of your forest floor; spring ephemerals bloom before the tree leaves emerge, and foliage plants carry on the show. Perennials grace water gardens and meadow and prairie plantings, and can be used as groundcovers. In all these settings, you can choose showy native plants to grow in addition to plants introduced from other lands. In fact, many world-famous perennials—purple coneflower, aster, phlox—are native to one or more of the floristic provinces that make up North America.

There are other compelling reasons to favor plants native to your area. Many plants have specific, symbiotic relationships with animals. Growing the appropriate larval and nectar plants for your area, for example, can help preserve or even reestablish an indigenous butterfly species whose habitat has been severely reduced by development.

By observing how native plants grow together in the wild, you can also create a plant community. A community is more than a collection of pretty perennials. It is an ecological grouping of plants growing in partnership with each other and their associated wildlife. Plant communities are self-sustaining, or close to it; once established, they need little in the way of water, fertilizer or other inputs. Few homeowners have the amount of land it takes to restore an entire native habitat, but it is possible to re-create plant communities to the best of our ability.

North America offers a breathtaking diversity of plant life, so gardening with just natives need not be limiting. What's more, many plant communities, including the prairie, and plants, such as cacti, are unique to the Americas.

NATIVE OR NATURALISTIC?

When you are designing a planting of perennials featuring natives, the first step is to decide whether you want an *informal, naturalistic planting* that combines native and non-native plants from all over the country or the world, or whether you want to make a bold statement with a *native plant garden* using only species from your floristic province. Some natural gardeners restrict their plant palette even further, to species indigenous to their immediate area (see "Choosing Native Perennials for Your Garden," page 8).

When the botanical world offers so many choices, it's not realistic to think that all gardeners are going to be satisfied by planting only natives. The degree to which you "go wild" is up to you. The only caveat: Never knowingly introduce an invasive plant to the landscape; invasive plants supplant native residents that may have supported a host of animals. And remember that only one plant can grow in one place at one time; because native habitat is shrinking rapidly, do not

By growing butterfly plants native to your area, you can help preserve species whose habitats have been reduced by development.

plant non-natives on wild or nearly wild land.

You might be surprised to find that a garden consisting solely of native plants isn't as limiting as you imagined. Some areas of North America have a breathtaking diversity of plant life. For example, it has been estimated that in the temperate world, the eastern United States is second only to China in botanical diversity. What's more, many areas of this continent are botanically unique. The prairie is a habitat found only in the United States and Canada. Cacti, too, are found only in the Americas. And within any one floristic province there are many different plant communities—wetland, upland, grassland, woodland. There are also hundreds of "niches" to choose from, micro-communities defined by topography and exposure—a rock outcropping, for instance, or a boggy area in your yard where rainwater collects. In any event, the many choices in gardening can be so overwhelming that limitations, like selecting plants that all have white flowers or, in this case, are all indigenous, can be helpful.

If you want to re-create a native plant community, you'll have to do some research. Find out what the area near your homesite was like in the years before settlement by European immigrants. Consult the map of floristic provinces on page 7; check at your local library, where there are often good records; purchase a guide to wild plants that is as specific to your area as possible; check the native plantings at local botanic gardens and arboreta. Then zero in on the plant communities that are most appropriate for the conditions on your property. If you live in the eastern deciduous forests province, for example, visit nearby woods in early spring to see the glorious perennials that grow and bloom there—trillium, Jack-in-the-pulpit, bloodroot. In your garden combine these plants within a herbaceous groundcover of perhaps *Geranium maculatum* or ferns. If you've chosen to create a naturalistic planting, then non-natives such as small-leaved epimediums or large hostas could also grow there.

Some examples of the many ways to use native perennials in a naturalistic design include: a spring woodland; a perennial border; an island bed; a shady border; a textural planting of individuals selected for their foliage shape and color; a groundcover of low-growing herbaceous plants such as the geranium; water's edge plantings; a herbaceous "bio-planting" with individuals chosen for their wildlife value—shelter and food in the form of fruit, pollen, nuts or seeds; and a meadow or prairie planting.

GARDEN ZONES

One commonsense way to decide where to grow native plants in your garden is to visualize your property as three different areas that reflect both your needs and the needs of the plants and animals that can flourish there.

From the garden zone closest to your home you can appreciate special collections and view the wild outer area beyond.

The *inner area* of your homesite is the high-traffic area with easy access to your house. This is a good place for entertaining, for example, and so it's usually covered in a hard surface like flagstone—unmortared to allow water to percolate downward and to provide habitat for soil dwellers. Raised decking makes a good choice for the hardscape of the inner area, both because it leaves the soil below unstressed and because it gets you up high, where you can look out into the native plantings beyond. The inner area is also an appropriate place for you to put special plant collections, preferably corralled by a fence or stone wall or other feature that sets them apart from the looser native landscape. Here you can cultivate exotic perennials under your watchful eye.

The *outer area*, often at the edges of your property, should be as wild as possible. This is often a good location for native plantings such as woodlands, shrubby areas that mix woody plants and perennials, or grasslands that consist of grasses and perennial wildflowers. These plantings can screen your property from neighbors or unsightly views and re-create natural habitat for beleaguered wildflowers and wildlife. Include plants that offer food for wildlife—plants with

17

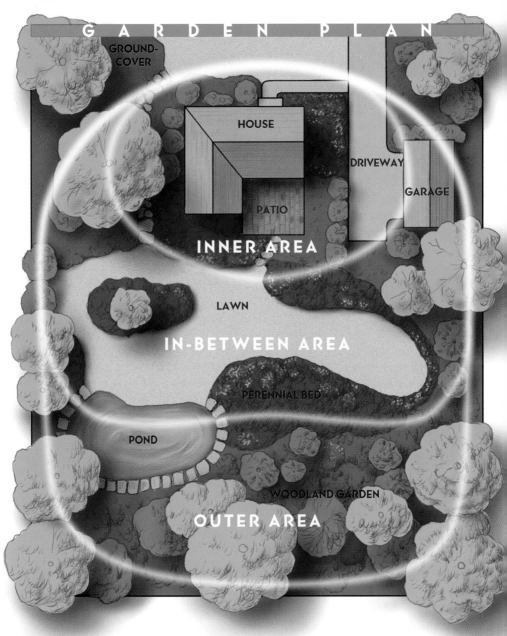

GARDEN PLAN

GROUND-COVER

HOUSE

DRIVEWAY

GARAGE

PATIO

INNER AREA

LAWN

IN-BETWEEN AREA

PERENNIAL BED

POND

WOODLAND GARDEN

OUTER AREA

In your garden's inner area you can cultivate exotic plants under your watchful eye. The in-between area can be the site of your most ambitious perennial creations. The wild outer area can screen your yard from the neighbors.

seeds, such as sunflowers; those with nectar, such as Joe-pye weed; those with heavy, rich pollen, such as goldenrod; and others, such as penstemons, with tubular red flowers to attract hummingbirds. It's also a good idea to include plants that provide shelter and nest material—those with dense, protective foliage in winter, such as native grasses, and ones with fluffy seedheads, such as *Clematis virginiana*.

The *in-between area*, which in the past might have contained a mix of lawn and ornamental islands or borders of non-native perennials, can be the principal area of interactive habitat—where you and the other garden residents, both plants and animals, will come into closest contact. This area could be the place for your most ambitious perennial creations, ideally reflecting your increased awareness of native varieties.

Devote some of your garden to a water element for moisture-loving native plants and wildlife.

Use this opportunity to reduce the size of your lawn, leaving only as much as you need for recreation. This saves not only on gasoline used for mowing, but also on water and petrochemical products such as fertilizers and pesticides.

Be sure, too, to include *a water element* in your garden. Aim to devote about 15 percent of your total landscape to some kind of wetland—pond, bog, wet meadow, stream or at the very least a significant garden pool. By the waterside, perennials that like wet feet, such as skunk cabbage and arrowhead, will be at home. Even in the desert, where 15 percent would be too much, wildlife will welcome some consistently available source of water.

You'll find that plantings made with indigenous perennials, or merely in the informal, naturalistic style, will attract a variety of wonderful birds and butterflies. Your creations bringing together many interdependent species—very unlike a conventional monoculture lawn—can be more than beautiful. They can directly benefit the beings who share your outdoor experience. And if you make your garden with an eye toward the health of the land—pesticide- and fungicide-free—it will be safer not only for the creatures but also for you and your family.

19

Growing Native Perennials

BY RUTH ROGERS CLAUSEN

GARDENING WITH NATIVE PLANTS requires as much attention to detail as growing plants from other parts of the world. As with any perennial, it's good horticultural practice to find out about a native plant's habitat and the kinds of conditions to which it is adapted in the wild. It is possible to manipulate certain conditions in the garden to re-create a plant's natural habitat, but the wisest course of action ecologically—and the one that involves the least work for you—is to choose plants that are suited to your site. For example, plants usually found in wet areas—blue vervain, meadow beauty, turtlehead, queen of the prairie, cardinal flower—are prime candidates for growing beside ponds, lakes and streams, where the soil seldom dries out, even in midsummer. Natives from the arid Southwest, such as blue flax, prairie coneflower and evening primroses, adapt well to gardens where little water is available.

PREPARING THE SOIL

Even plants that are well adapted to your conditions may benefit from improved soils. Many native perennials, especially those from woodland environments, such as green and gold, columbine and foamflower, do best in soil amended with compost or other organic matter. Again, the key is to be aware of the kind of soil found in a plant's native habitat. Black-eyed Susan, threadleaf coreopsis and other daisies found growing in the wild in rather poor, often dry soils may become tall and rangy and need to be staked in overly rich soils. In the garden as well as the wild, these plants do best in lean soil, relatively low in organic matter. Routine soil tests list the percentage of organic matter in the soil sample. In the East, for example, average soils contain 3 to 6 percent organic matter.

Gardening with natives requires as much attention to growing conditions as gardening with non-natives. Meadow beauty, top left, prefers constantly moist soil. Woodland natives foamflower, top right, and green and gold, bottom left, thrive in soil amended with organic matter. Black-eyed Susan, bottom right, likes poor soil.

Compacted soil, which is often inherited after new construction, must be broken up and amended with copious amounts of organic matter, unless you are planting species that enjoy a really lean soil. Ideally, prepare the soil at least a month or two prior to planting.

The level of organic matter in your soil isn't the only consideration. It's also important to know your soil's pH (acidity or alkalinity). Some plants such as trailing arbutus, rue anemone and Canada wild ginger grow naturally in highly acid soil and do poorly in alkaline soils, while others such as ostrich fern and Braun and mountain holly ferns require a sweet soil to grow well. Most plants are fairly flexible, though, and are happy with a soil pH of about 6 to 7. You can test your

WHERE TO GET NATIVE PERENNIALS

In recent years more and more nurseries have begun specializing in native plants. Many have handled perennials for a long time, but without singling out the natives. A large number of the well-loved perennials—asters, tickseeds, butterfly weed, foamflowers, penstemons, coralbells, common yarrow—are in fact native to this continent. Until recently, however, they were not advertised as such. Check at your local garden center for these popular plants. For more unusual varieties, see the list of nursery sources beginning on page 102.

Hundreds of thousands of native plants are propagated each year either from seed or by vegetative methods of division or cuttings, and are in no danger of extinction. But some of the most fervently sought after natives, including orchids and trilliums (see photo above), are difficult to propagate and have been collected from the wild to the point of endangerment. Part of the tragedy is that many wild-collected plants won't survive in a garden anyway, except under very special conditions.

Responsible gardeners should buy threatened native plants *only* from nurseries that propagate the plants they sell. Not all nurseries are equal in this respect. Some continue to dig endangered plants from the wild. A nursery can dig up a plant in the wild and then grow it for only a short time in order for it to qualify as "nursery grown." That is not the same as "nursery propagated." Fortunately, a growing number of excellent nurseries do in fact propagate their own material. The New England Wildflower Society publishes a booklet listing mail-order nurseries across the country that propagate their natives; for a copy, send $4.50 (which includes postage) to NEWS, 180 Hemenway Rd., Framingham, MA 01701.

What about the nurseries that are not listed? It is not out of line to ask nurserypeople where they get their stock. Ask if they propagate their natives themselves, dig plants from the wild or bring the stock in, and if so, where it comes from. Sometimes this information is not readily available, but it is important to keep asking. Boycott nurseries that offer wild-collected plants.

You can manipulate certain conditions in the garden to re-create those in a plant's wild habitat, but the wisest course of action ecologically—and the one that involves the least work for you—is to choose plants suited to your site. Blue vervain, left, grows naturally in wet areas; coneflower and blazingstar, right, in drier prairie sites.

soil pH yourself using one of the inexpensive test kits available at nurseries and garden centers, or send a soil sample to your local Cooperative Extension office or a professional soil-testing laboratory.

WORKING WITH THE WEATHER

As gardeners, we can control the soil to some extent, but we can't change the climate. Some Rocky Mountain species, like *Lewisia tweedyi,* thrive only where their native climate can be duplicated. Reliable snow cover is also important to some plants, especially those from mountain regions. They will tolerate any amount of cold in the winter when protected by a blanket of snow, but in regions such as the Northeast, where snow cover is unpredictable, these plants soon desiccate and die when exposed to icy winds. Plants native to southern California have evolved in the dry heat and Mediterranean climate of that region, and when transplanted to the same Zone 10 in Florida, they succumb to high humidity and heat.

Spring into early summer and late summer into fall are the best times to plant. Either season works well for most plants, although fall is preferable in regions where spring is short and followed rapidly by hot weather. Under these conditions, it may not be possible to keep spring transplants sufficiently moist for them to put out new roots into the still-cold surrounding soil. Fall planting takes advantage of warm soil, ideal for young root growth, but is less than ideal if your region is regularly subjected to long periods with drying winds, followed by severe early-winter weather. In parts of the West, fall is also a good time to plant because it is the rainy season.

MAINTENANCE

Although many native perennials require little attention once they are established, "low-maintenance" does not mean "no maintenance." You must still attend to the usual tasks of watering, feeding, staking, deadheading, mulching, winter protection, pest and disease control and cleaning up in spring and fall as necessary.

Clean-up is just another name for good garden hygiene: eliminating hiding places for pests and diseases, cutting back old stems to allow room for new growth, removing winter mulch and applying a summer mulch in spring and gently cultivating to break up the surface crustiness of the soil. Be sure to cultivate with great care, keeping an eye out for any young seedlings that can be potted and grown on until they are ready for planting in another part of the garden.

Proper plant selection and, when appropriate, soil preparation go a long way toward reducing the amount of irrigation required. When irrigation is necessary, though, it's wise to water deeply to encourage the roots to grow down toward moist soil. If you keep only the top couple of inches damp with daily sprinklings, you will encourage surface roots, which burn up rapidly in hot sun. Try to water at ground level early or late in the day to cut down on waste through evaporation.

Feed only when the plants show signs of a nutritional problem, such as yellowish or pale foliage and reduced vigor. The soft growth that results from overfeeding tends to be disease-prone and usually requires that the plants be staked. Grow native plants hard—prepare the soil well and then pretty much let them take care of themselves. If necessary, stake, as inconspicuously as possible, long before stems are flopping all over the place. Extend the blooming season by regular deadheading, unless you plan to collect seed. A summer mulch cuts down on weed growth, helps keep roots cool, reduces water loss by surface evaporation and looks pleasing. Organic materials such as buckwheat or cocoa hulls, pine needles, chopped leaves and shredded bark are good mulch materials for most plants, with the possible exception of those from the hot Southwest or the northern Rockies. These may prefer a gravel mulch, which ensures that moisture runs away fast and does not accumulate at the plants' crowns.

O KLAHOMA LEGISLATORS VOTED in 1986 to decree the blanket flower, a prairie wildflower native to the entire state, as the official State Wildflower. It already had mistletoe as its Floral Emblem, partly because, as Tulsa garden columnist Russell Studebaker put it, "other than red cedars, mistletoe is about the only thing green in the winter, so it's kinda nice to see."

Go figure. Steve Bender, a garden writer from Alabama, got in hot water for saying that mistletoe is the only thing that grows on Oklahoma's three trees. It was a poor joke on the Sooner State but made a point nevertheless: A floral emblem should be inspirational, not parasitic.

Ever notice how few states have wildflowers as their official flower? Some do, including Maryland (black-eyed Susan), Colorado (columbine) and Texas (bluebonnet). It made sense for Arizona to choose the magnificent giant saguaro cactus, and Mississippi to select the huge blossom of *Magnolia grandiflora*.

But what about the idea of having an official state *wild*flower? The National Wildflower Research Center, in Austin, Texas, doesn't keep records of those states that do—although they will gladly send you a listing of all the wildflower societies, in case you want to start a movement.

A movement—that's the idea! It's what happened in Mississippi, of all places. We were tired of having the magnolia as both our state flower *and* the state tree. So, the garden clubs of Mississippi, led by wildflower chairman Halla Jo Ellis, teamed up with kindred spirits for a unique idea: Why not have an official wildflower, too?

The reasoning for this ran the gamut from private agendas (a need to get the highway department to stop planting monocrops of California poppies) to the arcane (there's room for an extra symbol on the state map). Bottom line was, we needed to promote wildflowers, and this was as good a gimmick as any.

WANTED

Cardinal flower

Harebell

Primrose

Bee balm

STATES WILLING TO ADOPT THESE PLANTS AS THEIR FICIAL WILDFLOWERS

Butterfly weed

Ironweed

Phlox

Before it was over, the garden club ladies had narrowed the field, and the vote was close between Queen Anne's lace, a plant introduced from Europe, and black-eyed Susan, a short-lived perennial introduced in hay bales from the Midwest back in the 1880s. (One garden club nominated the Asian crape myrtle tree as our state "wildflower"— we have lots of education to do.)

But both were edged out by coreopsis—all species—and in 1990 it was named Mississippi's official State Wildflower. There were at least five good arguments for coreopsis: It's showy (and easy to draw and put on T-shirts); it's also a good cut flower, which is important if you're in a Mississippi garden club; several of its species are native to the state; it is a *garden-quality* plant readily available in the nursery trade and likely to be widely cultivated; and, if you'll excuse the cliché, last but not least, its seed can be sown in the fall by schoolchildren, and fresh seed harvested and saved the following spring—a very important consideration if wildflower promotion is on your agenda.

Of all those good reasons for selecting a native wildflower emblem for a state, the garden-quality one is the most crucial for marketing. That's how you make sure garden centers, wholesale growers, roadside managers, school kids and home gardeners will actually *use* it. I mean, who cares if a state flower is hardy and common, if it's an invasive agricultural weed that nobody can appreciate in their garden? Or so difficult to grow it's enjoyed only by hard-core hobbyists? What we need is a flower that kids and granddads and park managers alike can plant, roll around in and promote.

Take goldenrod: Not many gardeners will actively pursue it as a garden flower, because of its deserved reputation as a takeover artist. But the common, tall, field species isn't the only one available; there are many tidier, less invasive species that give a splash of color in the summer and fall garden. Look for the highly fragrant, licorice-leafed scented goldenrod *(Solidago odora)* and elmleaf goldenrod *(S. ulmifolia)* and cultivars galore. If your state had goldenrod as its wildflower emblem, you could easily enjoy petite goldenrods such as 'Cloth of Gold', 'Peter Pan', 'Golden Fleece', 'Crown of Rays' and 'Fireworks'. All are garden-friendly and attractive, good as cut flowers, pest-free, low-maintenance and *native*.

So, if your state has a native perennial as its floral emblem, do y'all grow it a lot on purpose? I know some night-time garden anarchists in Mississippi who once overseeded a highway department planting of California poppies and European cornflower with coreopsis seed—in effect "tainting" the fake wildflowers with the real stuff. And it worked.

My other question is, if your state does *not* have an official wildflower, can you see any reasons why it can't— soon?

OFFICIAL NATIVE FLORAL EMBLEMS

ALASKA	Forget-me-not
COLORADO	Columbine
HAWAII	Hibiscus
ILLINOIS	Violet
KANSAS	Sunflower
KENTUCKY	Goldenrod
MANITOBA	Pasqueflower
MARYLAND	Black-eyed Susan
MINNESOTA	Lady's slipper orchid
MISSISSIPPI	Coreopsis
MONTANA	Bitterroot
NEBRASKA	Goldenrod
NEW BRUNSWICK	Purple violet
NEWFOUNDLAND	Pitcher plant
NEW JERSEY	Violet
NEW MEXICO	Yucca
ONTARIO	White trillium
PRINCE EDWARD ISLAND	Lady's slipper orchid
RHODE ISLAND	Purple violet
SASKATCHEWAN	Prairie lily
SOUTH DAKOTA	American pasqueflower
UTAH	Sego lily
WISCONSIN	Woods violet
YUKON	Fireweed

(from the *World Book Encyclopedia*)

ENCYCLOPEDIA OF NATIVE PERENNIALS

EASTERN DECIDUOUS FORESTS

COASTAL PLAIN

CENTRAL PRAIRIES & PLAINS

WESTERN MOUNTAINS & PACIFIC NORTHWEST

WESTERN DESERTS

CALIFORNIA

In the following encyclopedia, six leading horticulturists each describe a dozen spectacular wildflowers native to the floristic province in which they live (see map on page 7). You can find the section on each province by following the colored tabs, illustrated at right.

Eastern Deciduous Forests
by Juliet A. Hubbard

Coastal Plain
by Ken Moore

Central Prairies and Plains
by C. Colston Burrell

Western Mountains and Pacific Northwest
by Gayle Weinstein

Western Deserts
by Judith Phillips

California
by Bob Perry

Aster novae-angliae

NEW ENGLAND ASTER

NATIVE HABITAT: Throughout the eastern United States in rich, moist meadows.

HARDINESS ZONE: USDA 4-8, Sunset all zones

OUTSTANDING FEATURES: Great clusters of yellow-eyed flowers come in vibrant hues of rose, pink and violet, and bring a grand finale of color to the autumn garden. Spectacular in fall cut-flower arrangements as well.

HABIT AND GARDEN USE: These tough, dependable plants can be used in perennial borders, cut-flower gardens or as color accents in foundation plantings. Most grow 4' to 5' tall, so should be planted in the middle or back of the border. For arrangements, cut blossoms 24 hours before use, as flowers close and reopen after a day's rest.

HOW TO GROW: Grow in full sun in moderately moist and rich soil. Taller forms may need staking to support the weight of the flowers. Transplant in spring or in fall after flowering.

CULTIVARS AND RELATED SPECIES:
'Harrington's Pink'—Clear salmon-pink, 4'.
'Alma Potschke'—Hot rose, 3'.
'Hella Lacy'—Violet-blue, 4' to 5'.
'Purple Dome'—Vibrant purple, 18".
A. umbellatus, flat-topped aster—Clouds of white flowers lightly touched with pale yellow, 5'.

Eupatorium maculatum

JOE-PYE WEED

NATIVE HABITAT: Grows naturally in moist, sunny meadows and alongside streams throughout eastern North America.

HARDINESS ZONE: USDA 4-9, Sunset all zones

OUTSTANDING FEATURES: Joe-pye weed is named after a 19th-century healer who used this plant in many of his cures. Its huge, dome-shaped clusters of dusty rose flowers are held magnificently aloft at 5' to 7' in late summer, and deep green leaves are dramatically arranged in tiered whorls. This common roadside wildflower is less appreciated in the U.S. than in Europe, where it is often given a place of honor in perennial borders.

HABIT AND GARDEN USE: This plant needs plenty of space to reach its full potential. Place it in the back of the garden 4' away from other plants. Joe-pye weed can be used in perennial borders and is also lovely combined with ornamental grasses.

HOW TO GROW: In cultivation, *Eupatorium* prefers a rich, moist soil in full sun, as it does in the wild. In drier conditions it will not grow as tall. Transplants easily in spring or fall.

CULTIVARS AND RELATED SPECIES:
'Gateway'—Large, wine-red blossoms.
'Atropurpureum'—Deep purple-rose flowers; purple-red stems heighten the architectural effect of the leaves.

31

Heuchera americana

ALUMROOT

NATIVE HABITAT: Found in rocky woods, with its roots growing in pockets of moist, humus-rich soil throughout eastern North America.

HARDINESS ZONE: USDA 4-9, Sunset 2-24

OUTSTANDING FEATURES: Large ornamental evergreen leaves have maple-like shape and often touches of gray or red. Many exciting new forms are being introduced, with various marbled patterns in green, gray and red.

HABIT AND GARDEN USE: Bold leaves form 18" mounds, which can be planted closely together to form a dense evergreen groundcover. Airy white flowers in summer add a light and graceful note. Red-leaved plants make a useful accent in a perennial border or a foundation planting, while gray and red marbled forms offer new colors and textures for use as groundcovers in shade or sun.

HOW TO GROW: Heucheras are tolerant of dry to moderately moist soil and full sun to light shade. In hotter climates the plants will require some shade. They may be transplanted in spring or fall.

CULTIVARS AND RELATED SPECIES:
'Dale's Strain'—Grown from seed, the leaves of these plants come in a variety of patterns of green, red and gray.
H. micrantha var. *diversifolia* 'Palace Purple'—Deep purple leaves combine beautifully with many flower colors.

Heuchera americana 'Dale's Strain'

Hibiscus moscheutos (H. palustris)

ROSE MALLOW

NATIVE HABITAT: Found primarily along the coast of the eastern United States in fresh-water marshes.

HARDINESS ZONE: USDA 4-9, Sunset 7-24

OUTSTANDING FEATURES: Huge, cupped blossoms of pink, rose or white are a bright yet graceful accent to the summer garden, lending a slightly tropical appearance—and the broad leaves and large blossoms provide contrast to other plants.

HABIT AND GARDEN USE: Grows 5' tall and wide. With its commanding presence, it can stand alone as a specimen plant, yet works equally well in perennial borders, foundation plantings or mixed in with shrubs. The seedpods and flower stalks remain interesting and decorative all winter long.

HOW TO GROW: Rose mallow grows naturally in moist, somewhat sandy sites, yet it is amazingly adaptable as long as it receives full sun. It can grow in poorly drained areas or fairly dry gardens. Plants start late in the spring, then appear to

grow 6" a day until they begin flowering in July. No staking is necessary. Plants may be moved in spring or fall.

CULTIVARS AND RELATED SPECIES:
H. 'Southern Belle'—Seed-grown mix of red, pink or white flowers larger and flatter than the species.
H. 'Disco Belle'—Full-size flowers in red, pink or white on dwarf, 2' to 3' plants.
H. 'Lord Baltimore'—Big, red, ruffled flowers, 5' tall.

Lobelia siphilitica

GREAT BLUE LOBELIA

NATIVE HABITAT: Swamps, alongside streams and in moist meadows throughout North America.

HARDINESS ZONE: USDA 4-9, Sunset 1-7, 12-17

OUTSTANDING FEATURES: The vivid columns of the great blue lobelia provide much needed blue to late summer and fall gardens. Exciting hybrids have been made between this species and red *L. cardinalis* ranging from white, to pink, to deep red, to violet.

HABIT AND GARDEN USE: Forms low rosettes from which flower spikes arise. Lovely intermingled with other flowers in a perennial border. It is not long-lived, but will self-sow profusely, spreading its progeny throughout the garden.

HOW TO GROW: Prefers light shade and a rich moist soil but will also grow in sun in average soil. In shade the flower spikes are taller, up to 4', while in sun the flower spikes will be shorter, about 2' tall, but more profuse. Plants may be moved in spring or fall.

CULTIVARS AND RELATED SPECIES:
L. siphilitica 'Alba'—White-flowered form.
L. cardinalis, cardinal flower—See page 50.

Monarda didyma

BEE BALM

NATIVE HABITAT: Moist, partially shaded areas along streams and in moist meadows throughout eastern North America.

HARDINESS ZONE: USDA 4-9, Sunset all zones

OUTSTANDING FEATURES: Clusters of tubular flowers in jewel tones of pink, violet and red attract hummingbirds as well as humans. Its fragrant leaves impart the superb flavor and aroma to Earl Grey tea, and the flowers of bee balm are also beautiful when dried.

HABIT AND GARDEN USE: Monardas form 3' mounds of color in the summer and look beautiful in the middle of perennial and herb gardens. They are also useful as a color accent in foundation plantings.

HOW TO GROW: All monardas prefer full sun and rich, moist soil. In parts of the country with high humidity, place the plants in areas with good air circulation,

where foliage is less likely to mildew. (The cultivars listed below have been selected for their mildew resistance as well as their brilliant color.) Plant in spring or fall; bee balm is easily divided at these times as well.

CULTIVARS AND RELATED SPECIES:
M. 'Adam'—A rich red, 2-1/2' tall.
M. 'Blue Stocking'—Lovely violet-blue.
M. 'Mahogany'—Deep red blossoms.
M. 'Marshall's Delight'—Clear rose-pink.

Panicum virgatum

SWITCH GRASS

NATIVE HABITAT: Both dry and moist meadows and prairies throughout North America.

HARDINESS ZONE: USDA 3-8, Sunset 3-24

OUTSTANDING FEATURES: Light and airy seed heads held aloft above fine 3' foliage provide the perfect foil to late-summer– and fall-blooming flowers. This lovely and tough plant is even more garden-worthy with the introduction of the variety 'Hänse Herms'; its foliage turns a vivid deep red in late summer and retains the color through fall.

HABIT AND GARDEN USE: Useful as a specimen among other perennials or in a mass planting. Its adaptability to adverse conditions makes it a useful landscape plant—perhaps a nice substitute for the overused groundcover, juniper. Birds enjoy the seeds, making this a good plant for wildlife gardens.

HOW TO GROW: Switch grass is best in full sun, although tolerant of light shade. It can grow in dry or moist conditions. Transplant and divide in spring only.

CULTIVARS AND RELATED SPECIES:
'Heavy Metal'—Distinct bluish color to the foliage, 4'.
'Hänse Herms'—Foliage turns deep red in fall, 3'.

Phlox divaricata

WOODLAND PHLOX

NATIVE HABITAT: Rich open woods throughout eastern North America.

HARDINESS ZONE: USDA 3-8, Sunset 1-17

OUTSTANDING FEATURES: Less well-known than its cousin the tall garden phlox, this diminutive beauty bursts forth in spring with dramatic sky-blue blossoms, which release a faint perfume to the air. This fragrant carpet of blue lasts for a month, creating an unforgettable paradise when combined with dogwoods and native azaleas in a woodland garden.

HABIT AND GARDEN USE: Individual plants form 1', slowly creeping mounds. Correctly sited, woodland phlox will slowly seed itself about, creating great masses of color. It is not very noticeable out of bloom, so should be interplanted with bolder-leaved plants such as ferns, Solomon's seal, astilbes and hostas to give the garden texture and interest in summer and fall.

HOW TO GROW: Woodland phlox prefers a rich, moderately moist soil and sun-dappled shade. It is easily transplanted in spring or fall. If seedlings are not desired, plants can be cut back after blooming. Mildew is rarely a problem, but if it does appear in very hot and humid climates, prune back unsightly foliage.

CULTIVARS AND RELATED SPECIES:
'London Grove Blue'—Large fragrant blue flowers.
'Fuller's White'—Intoxicatingly fragrant white blossoms.

P. paniculata, garden phlox—Great masses of fragrant, dome-shaped flowers, 3' to 4'. Cultivars in a range of flower colors.
P. maculata (P. carolina), garden phlox—Slightly smaller than the above, with striking conical inflorescences. Foliage is mildew resistant. 'Miss Lingard' bears waxy white flowers in June.
P. stolonifera—Spring blooming, with ground-hugging foliage and showy drifts of blossoms. Blue-, white-, pink- and purple-flowered forms are available.

Porteranthus (Gillenia) trifoliatus

BOWMAN'S ROOT

NATIVE HABITAT: Rich woods throughout eastern North America.

HARDINESS ZONE: USDA 4-8, Sunset 2-24

OUTSTANDING FEATURES: Starry, butterfly-like flowers cloak this plant in airy white from head to toe for three to four weeks in mid-spring. Its ornamental, deep green, three-parted leaves remain glossy all summer and take on a reddish tint in the fall.

HABIT AND GARDEN USE: Bowman's root forms a giant 4' mound when mature. Because of its size and interesting foliage, it can be used as a key design element in a herbaceous planting, or in a mixed shrub border or foundation planting. Its baby's breath–like appearance is particularly enchanting combined with roses.

HOW TO GROW: Although this plant grows in woodlands in the wild, it reaches its greatest potential when grown in full sun to light shade and a rich, moderately moist soil. In hotter climates give it a half day of shade. Transplant in spring or fall, and cut back stems in late fall or early spring before the new growth appears.

CULTIVARS AND RELATED SPECIES:
P. stipulatus, Indian physic— More upright than the mounding bowman's root, and flowers two weeks later. Glossy five-parted leaves resemble a Japanese cut-leaf maple and turn exquisite deep red in fall.

Rudbeckia laciniata

CUTLEAF CONEFLOWER

NATIVE HABITAT: Rich moist sites, often along streambanks throughout North America.

HARDINESS ZONE: USDA 3-9, Sunset all zones

OUTSTANDING FEATURES: This big, free-flowering summer bloomer bears a multitude of flowers composed of drooping lemon-yellow petals surrounding green cones. Several special selections with larger or shaggy double flowers are growing more popular every day.

HABIT AND GARDEN USE: *Rudbeckia laciniata* grows 5' to 8' tall, depending on soil moisture, and works well in the back of the border where its flowers attract the attention of butterflies as well as humans. Shorter selections, such as 'Goldquelle', are suitable in the middle of a perennial border.

HOW TO GROW: *Rudbeckia laciniata* prefers a sunny spot in rich, moist soil,

although it will also grow with moderate moisture. Plants may be moved in spring or fall and do not need staking when grown in full sun.

CULTIVARS AND RELATED SPECIES: 'Goldquelle' ('Well of Gold')—Shaggy, double yellow flowers on a shorter 3' plant.
'Hortensia' ('Golden Glow')—Introduced in 1894 and still commonly seen around old homesteads; 5' to 6' tall with double yellow blossoms.
R. nitida 'Herbstsonne' ('Autumn Sun')—Despite the name, this plant flowers all summer long; 6' to 7' tall with larger, showier foliage and flowers than the species.

Stylophorum diphyllum

WOOD POPPY

NATIVE HABITAT: Rich woods throughout central and southeastern United States.

HARDINESS ZONE: USDA 4-9, Sunset 3-24

OUTSTANDING FEATURES: A harbinger of spring, the showy yellow blossoms of this plant brighten woodland gardens like a native version of the daffodil. Large boldly lobed leaves offer a nice textural contrast to other spring-flowering plants; with woodland phlox it forms a breathtaking sea of yellow and blue. It is a thrifty gardener's delight, for even one plant will quickly naturalize and weave itself throughout the garden.

HABIT AND GARDEN USE: This plant begins blooming in early spring, soon after it emerges from the ground, and continues flowering as it grows to its final size of 2-1/2' to 3' tall and half as wide. Wood poppy spreads vigorously from seed so is best suited to large shade gardens where a showy, quickly-spreading, low-maintenance plant is needed. Unwanted seedlings are easily pulled or transplanted to new locations. Combine with ferns, blue woodland phlox and Solomon's seal.

HOW TO GROW: Wood poppies do best in a moist rich soil and partial shade. Seedlings may be easily transplanted in spring or fall, or pick dry seedpods in late spring and early summer and sprinkle seeds around the garden. Seedlings will appear the following spring. In dry soils or hot climates, plants may look ragged or go dormant in mid-summer; place toward the back of the garden near other plants that have good-looking foliage throughout the season.

CULTIVARS AND RELATED SPECIES: Do not confuse with *Chelidonium majus*, European wood poppy, a tenacious weed in the U.S., with smaller yellow flowers and less ornamental foliage.

FOAMFLOWER

NATIVE HABITAT: Rich woods, primarily in the mountains, throughout eastern North America.

HARDINESS ZONE: USDA 3-8, Sunset 1-9, 14-24

OUTSTANDING FEATURES: Low spikes of starry white flowers densely carpet the forest floor in spring, resembling a blanket of foam—hence the name. This rapidly creeping groundcover grows well in light to fairly dense shade. In warmer climates, bronze-tinged foliage remains evergreen; in colder climates, without snowcover, plant is evergreen about half the winter.

HABIT AND GARDEN USE: *Tiarella* grows only 4" high, with flower spikes to 8". It creeps rapidly, sending out long runners that soon root. Foamflower is not invasive and will wend itself among other spring-blooming woodland plants such as *Phlox divaricata* and *Stylophorum diphyllum,* creating a tapestry of blue, yellow and white.

Tiarella cordifolia var. *collina*

HOW TO GROW: Grows best in a moderately moist, lightly shaded site. Soil should be rich in organic matter, such as rotted leaves or compost. Plants may be moved in spring or fall.

CULTIVARS AND RELATED SPECIES: 'Slickrock'—Finely cut leaves, light pink-white flowers. Very vigorous. *T. cordifolia* var. *collina* (*T. wherryi*)—Larger southern form with light pink flowers; non-creeping. 'Oakleaf'—Leaves shaped like miniature oak leaves.

WILD COLUMBINE

NATIVE HABITAT: Well-drained soils of open, sunny woodlands and woodland edges from the Northeast west to Minnesota; south to Florida and Texas.

HARDINESS ZONE: USDA 4, Sunset all zones

OUTSTANDING FEATURES: Lush lettuce-green foliage in late winter (all winter in milder areas) is followed in early spring by yellow and red flowers, which bloom over two to four weeks. Flowers appear to dangle in midair, attracting early arriving hummingbirds.

HABIT AND GARDEN USE: Spring-flowering stems reach 1-1/2' to 2-1/2' from a basal mound, which persists most of the growing season. Use as a specimen or accent plant—against rocks, tree stumps, edges of steps or along garden paths—or in mass plantings spaced throughout a woodland garden with ferns and other shade-lovers. Especially attractive with spring phlox, *Phacelia* and foamflower.

HOW TO GROW: Grows in full shade to full sun but performs best with filtered sunlight or afternoon shade. For robust foliage and flowering, a sunny location with humus-rich, well-drained soil and supplementary watering during drought is best.

CULTIVARS AND RELATED SPECIES:
Natural seedlings often produce attractive color variants including pale red, pink, and pale yellow to almost white.

JACK-IN-THE-PULPIT

NATIVE HABITAT: Alluvial forests and boggy areas of mixed deciduous woodland slopes from the Northeast west to North Dakota; south to Florida and Texas.

HARDINESS ZONE: USDA 4, Sunset 4-17

OUTSTANDING FEATURES: In mid-spring, this plant makes a dramatic, one- to two-week long emergence from the ground as a sharp pointed spike. Its leaves soon unfurl, sheltering a hooded enclosure (the spathe), which contains the rounded dowel-shaped extension of the spadix—the preacher, "Jack," in a pulpit. Perhaps more outstanding is the cluster of brilliant red berry-like fruit (only on female, "Jill," plants), held aloft after the leaves have shrunken away, making a bold effect in the woodland garden in late summer.

HABIT AND GARDEN USE: Plants grow from a corm to 1' to 1-1/2', and can be quite long-lived and produce numerous seedlings. The striking three-lobed leaf, two per mature plant, are handsome in the shade or woodland garden between flowering and fruiting. A single plant makes a nice effect emerging through a low groundcover or situated against a stone or contrasting foliage background. A

group of Jack-in-the-pulpits along a garden path, and particularly on a slope at eye level, will never cease to stop visitors in their tracks.

HOW TO GROW: Perfect for a permanently moist spot in the shade and can even tolerate direct morning sunlight. In the South, even with constant moisture, provide protection from afternoon sun. Can be grown well in any woodland garden as long as soil is humus-rich and kept moist.

CULTIVARS AND RELATED SPECIES: Watch for naturally occurring variations in spathe color from pale green to black-and-green striped.

Asclepias tuberosa

BUTTERFLY WEED

NATIVE HABITAT: Roadsides, prairies, fields and forest edges from the Northeast west to Minnesota and south to Florida.

HARDINESS ZONE: USDA 4, Sunset all zones

OUTSTANDING FEATURES: Brilliant orange flowers cover this drought-resistant perennial in mid-summer and attract butterflies.

HABIT AND GARDEN USE: Plants reach height and breadth of 1' to 2'. Best displayed as a specimen plant in the front to midsection of a perennial border or island bed. Deadheading the first bloom results in a second flowering. One of the best plants to establish in a meadow-like area or yard that is infrequently mowed.

HOW TO GROW: Requires at least half a day of full sunlight and a well-drained location. Mature plants don't transplant well so plant as a seedling or small container plant where it will remain; plants reach full size in two to four years. Plant breaks dormancy very slowly in spring; mark its location before it dies back to avoid damaging it.

CULTIVARS AND RELATED SPECIES:
Be on the lookout for various unnamed color forms— pale sulfur yellow through bright orange to almost crimson red—which are frequently described and offered by nurseries.

Baptisia alba

WILD WHITE INDIGO

NATIVE HABITAT: Dry sandy woods, savannas and prairie-like habitats from Virginia south to Georgia, west Florida, Alabama and eastern Tennessee.

HARDINESS ZONE: USDA 7 (probably safe to 5), Sunset all zones

OUTSTANDING FEATURES: One of the most striking mid-spring plants as it emerges—it looks like black-stemmed asparagus with white flower tips showing from charcoal-colored buds—it never ceases to attract attention. Erect spires of pure white, lupine-like flowers are held above waxy, trifoliate foliage. No pest or disease problems.

HABIT AND GARDEN USE: This upright, shrub-like perennial can reach over 3' tall and 2' to 3' in breadth. Best situated singly or in groups at the middle of the

perennial border, where shorter plants will be displayed to advantage against its handsome foliage. Locate at least one specimen up front, for a close view of the emerging flowering stems.

HOW TO GROW: Obtain as a small seedling, as plant quickly develops a robust, multi-taproot-like system that makes it very drought tolerant. Place plant where you want it to remain. It will not flower the first year but will become more robust each year and will eventually have a dozen or so flowering stems. Grow in well-drained soil and at least half a day of sun.

CULTIVARS AND RELATED SPECIES:
B. x 'Purple Smoke'—A purplish blue-flowered hybrid between the blue-flowered *B. australis* and *B. alba.* Introduced by the North Carolina Botanical Garden and Niche Gardens of Chapel Hill, North Carolina.

COASTAL PLAIN

45

Geranium maculatum

WILD GERANIUM

NATIVE HABITAT: Mixed deciduous woodlands from Maine to Nebraska and Oklahoma, and south to South Carolina, northern Georgia and Arkansas.

HARDINESS ZONE: USDA 4, Sunset 4-17

OUTSTANDING FEATURES: A sophisticated and unanticipated surprise in the woodland garden and in more conventional perennial borders. An attractive mound of dark green, rough-textured, palmately lobed foliage appears in early spring, followed by quarter-size, five-petaled, blue to purplish flowers.

HABIT AND GARDEN USE: Plant is dramatic as an accent, singly or in small groupings. This clump-forming perennial holds flowers 1-1/2' to 2' high on sparsely branched stems. Create a magical display by spreading it throughout a woodland garden, perhaps mixed with wild columbine, to provide a dancing effect as flowers hang above the ground.

HOW TO GROW: Grows best in humus-rich, moist, but well-drained soil with filtered sunlight. To ensure attractive mounds of foliage and heavy flowering, provide ample moisture during drought periods and add organic compost at least annually. Protect from the harsh afternoon sunlight in sunnier locations.

CULTIVARS AND RELATED SPECIES: Look for subtle color variations from pale, almost pink flowers to dark blue, almost purple flowers as plants self-sow in garden.

SWAMP SUNFLOWER

NATIVE HABITAT: Savannas, ditches, wet meadows and pine barrens from New York west to Oklahoma and south to Florida and Texas.

HARDINESS ZONE: USDA 6, Sunset all zones

OUTSTANDING FEATURES: Late fall-flowering *Helianthus* holds almost iridescent golden orange flowers high above the ground. A real knockout in the fall perennial border.

HABIT AND GARDEN USE: This very tall (up to 8'), long-lived plant has rough, willow leaf–like foliage. Situate at the rear of perennial border, island bed or wild meadow garden, where you want a dramatic glow at the very end of the growing season. For a special effect, plant ornamental morning glories or let naturalized morning glories run freely up this tall perennial.

HOW TO GROW: Cultivate in any good garden soil in full sun, and water during

prolonged droughts. Will better withstand dry conditions if established in a wild meadow garden (not hard clay, however), but flowering will be less exuberant than in a cultivated setting. Prune during mid-season to reduce its height, otherwise stake it early to prevent it from flopping just before it puts on its show. Nursery plants tend to be more robust than those in the wild.

CULTIVARS AND RELATED SPECIES:
No named cultivars.

Kosteletzkya virginica

SEASHORE MALLOW

NATIVE HABITAT: Edges of coastal rivers and marshes from Long Island south to Florida and Texas.

HARDINESS ZONE: USDA 6, Sunset 5-24

OUTSTANDING FEATURES: Though restricted in the wild to brackish wet margins, this is, surprisingly, one of the most sun-loving and drought-resistant of all native perennials. Lovely pink flowers bloom in late summer and fall, attracting butterflies. The rough pubescent yellow-green, halberd-shaped leaves are not bothered by insect pests as are other native mallows.

HABIT AND GARDEN USE: Plant can attain a height of over 6' (up to 8') and a spread of 6', so place at the rear of the garden and give each specimen ample room. Situate where you wish to attract butterflies, or use as a background hedge on large grounds. Flowers remain fully open on overcast or cool sunny days or with afternoon shade, but on hot sunny days they tend to wither by early afternoon.

HOW TO GROW: Site in any naturally wet sunny areas in the garden or wild landscape. However, the plant is extremely drought tolerant, and performs well in prepared garden soil with mulch at the base. Breaks dormancy very late in spring, so mark it to avoid damage during spring gardening activities. After three to five years, plants tend to play out and it's best to replant.

CULTIVARS AND RELATED SPECIES: No named cultivars. White-flowered forms are available from nurseries in the Deep South, but they can hardly compare with this beautiful pink one.

BLAZING STAR

NATIVE HABITAT: Savannas, bogs and wet meadows from New York west to southeastern Wisconsin and south to Florida and Louisiana.

HARDINESS ZONE: USDA 5, Sunset 1-10, 14-24

OUTSTANDING FEATURES: Tall purple-flowering spires create a spectacular effect in the late summer and fall garden against the yellows and whites of other late-flowering plants.

HABIT AND GARDEN USE: Flowering stems of blazing star begin as grasslike clumps from corms, and will grow 4' to 6' in a sunny perennial border or open meadow garden. Stake plants early, as they become top-heavy with flowers. Place at rear of flower borders and center of island beds, and in large beds repeat them as specimens or in small groups.

HOW TO GROW: Full sun and moist, sandy or humus-rich soil is best. In drier conditions, supplement watering to maintain robustness. Heavy clay soil requires considerable amending.

CULTIVARS AND RELATED SPECIES:
L. elegans and *L. pycnostachya,* similar to *L. spicata,* are tall, purple-flowered species.

Lobelia cardinalis

CARDINAL FLOWER

NATIVE HABITAT: Wet ditches and edges of streams, rivers and ponds from the Northeast west to Minnesota and south to Florida and eastern Texas.

HARDINESS ZONE: USDA 4, Sunset 1-7, 12-17

OUTSTANDING FEATURES: The color of the cardinal flower is perhaps the most beautiful red in nature; it also attracts hummingbirds. It is one of the easiest and most rewarding plants to cultivate, once you learn its tricks.

HABIT AND GARDEN USE: Vigorous leafy flower stems grow from an evergreen basal rosette, reaching a height of 4' to 6' in good conditions and flowering from early July through September. Situate several clumps in shade at the edge of an open landscape, where filtered rays of sunlight highlight the flowers, or scatter throughout borders, along the edge of a patio or below a raised deck to attract hummingbirds.

HOW TO GROW: This versatile wildflower grows in full shade or full sun, in continuously wet or moist areas—take advantage of a leaky air conditioner, faucet or birdbath. It also responds to any good garden soil when watered during dry periods. Plant readily self-seeds, even in moist lawns. The basal rosettes, which develop at the base of fruiting stems, grow actively under winter sunlight. Make sure they are not covered with mulch or hidden under natural leaf fall during the winter, or they will die. In colder regions, mulch carefully around the plants and replant if heaved out of the ground by hard freezes.

CULTIVARS AND RELATED SPECIES:
Most nurseries offer white and pink forms with a variety of names and hybrids with dark burgundy foliage. Blue-flowered *Lobelia siphilitica* (see page 34) contrasts nicely with the reds and is easily cultivated with them.

HORSEMINT

NATIVE HABITAT: Dry, sandy roadsides or fields and woodland edges from Vermont west to Minnesota and south to Florida and Texas.

HARDINESS ZONE: USDA 4, Sunset all zones

OUTSTANDING FEATURES: Yellow flowers spotted with brown, nestled above pink-colored bracts, are unusual and particularly striking when placed in a flower arrangement.

HABIT AND GARDEN USE: This long-lived perennial is loosely erect and often sprawling, reaching a height of 1' to 2'. Best appreciated as a container plant on a deck or patio, where its exquisite flowers can most easily be enjoyed at close range. Or situate in small groups in perennial borders, where its vigorous response to improved soil and moisture will necessitate staking, or establish it in a wild meadow garden.

HOW TO GROW: Grows best in sunny locations with some shade; the beauty of its flowers and bracts is lost in the harsh light of the afternoon summer sun. It is drought tolerant but does well if given a good garden soil and extra moisture during dry periods.

CULTIVARS AND RELATED SPECIES: None.

BLACK-EYED SUSAN

NATIVE HABITAT: Various prairie, field and roadside habitats scattered essentially throughout the U.S.

HARDINESS ZONE: USDA 4, Sunset all zones

OUTSTANDING FEATURES: Bright orange-yellow flowers with dark centers brighten up the garden and are particularly at home in the wild meadow garden. Also a great cut flower. It spreads rather successfully by seed, even into the lawn.

HABIT AND GARDEN USE: In the wild sunny garden this short-lived perennial reaches a height of 1' to 1-1/2', and flowers early to mid-summer. In the improved soil and moisture conditions of cultivated garden beds and borders, it can become twice as tall, quite robust and will flop over if not staked. Once established, it will move about freely on its own.

HOW TO GROW: Black-eyed Susan needs at least half a day of sunlight for good performance. As with most wildflowers in cultivation, where soil texture, fertility and moisture content are more favorable than in the wild, this plant will grow larger, produce more flowers and come to depend on additional watering. To establish it in a low-maintenance, meadow-like garden, plant young seedlings in the fall or very early spring.

CULTIVARS AND RELATED SPECIES: *R. fulgida* 'Goldsturm'—Extensive mats of dark green foliage with persistent yellow-orange flowers for three to six weeks from mid- to late summer.
R. fulgida—Forms clumps rather than mats; flowers are smaller and in a more open flowering mass, from late summer to fall.

Solidago rugosa, S. odora, S. sempervirens

ROUGH-LEAF, FRAGRANT & SEASIDE GOLDENRODS

NATIVE HABITAT: Roadsides, savannas, pine barrens and meadows from the Northeast west to Minnesota and south to Florida and Texas. Seaside goldenrod is found on coastal sand dunes and edges of brackish marshes from the Northeast south to the Gulf states.

HARDINESS ZONE: USDA 6, Sunset all zones

OUTSTANDING FEATURES: These three distinctively different goldenrods are choice garden plants and non-invasive. The beautiful yellow summer and fall flowers do not cause hay fever and enhance any cultivated or wild garden.

HABIT AND GARDEN USE: Fragrant and seaside goldenrods are clump formers; rough-leaf goldenrod develops a mat of foliage (evergreen in milder southern regions) resembling ajuga in winter months. Flower heads of fragrant goldenrod are pyramidal spires on 1-1/2'- to 4'-high stems. Seaside goldenrod has narrower pyramidal flower heads, 2' to 4' high. Flowering branches of rough-leaf goldenrod are generally 1-1/2' to 3' high. All are best displayed in sunny borders to contrast with the blues and whites of summer and fall flowers.

Solidago rugosa 'Fireworks'

HOW TO GROW: All are easily cultivated in good garden soil and survive well in droughts. Keep seaside goldenrod on the dry side, otherwise it will require staking. For best growth of fragrant and rough-leaf goldenrods, water during very dry periods.

CULTIVARS AND RELATED SPECIES: *S. rugosa* 'Fireworks'—An elegant lacy, horizontal form unlike typical goldenrods.

Aster oblongifolius

AROMATIC ASTER

NATIVE HABITAT: Dry, sandy to rocky slopes in prairies, meadows, open woods and savannas from Pennsylvania to Saskatchewan, south to Alabama and New Mexico.

HARDINESS ZONE: USDA 3-8, Sunset all zones

OUTSTANDING FEATURES: Mounds of 1-1/4" purple flowers cover the 16" stems of this overlooked aster in mid-autumn. A real showstopper, this outstanding plant blooms for at least three weeks in September and early October. Fuzzy, oblong foliage and scaly buds create an interesting display through the summer season.

HABIT AND GARDEN USE: Plants spread by creeping, fibrous-rooted rhizomes to form dense, broad clumps. At bloom time, clumps exhibit a loose habit and open form. Perfect for meadows, prairies and exuberant perennial beds; combine aromatic aster with grasses, goldenrod, sunflower and anemone.

HOW TO GROW: Give plants average, well-drained soil in full sun or light shade. Plants flop miserably in too much shade or rich soils. Divide clumps in early spring or after flowering. Tip cuttings root easily in early summer. Foliage is somewhat susceptible to powdery mildew.

CULTIVARS AND RELATED SPECIES:
'Dream of Beauty'—Selected by guru of Great Plains flora Claude Barr, this cultivar is shorter in stature and has rose-pink flowers.
'Raydon's Favorite'—A southern cultivar with blue-purple flowers.

PURPLE PRAIRIE CLOVER

NATIVE HABITAT: Moist to seasonally wet black-soil prairies in full sun, and occasionally drier, sandy sites; from Illinois and Montana, south to Alabama and New Mexico.

HARDINESS ZONE: USDA 3-9, Sunset 12-13

OUTSTANDING FEATURES: Dense, elongated 1" to 3" clover-like spikes of small purple flowers attract bees and butterflies, and add an airy exclamation of sparkling purple to the early summer garden. Flashy, fountain-like clumps are heavily weighted with blooms. Like all legumes, these fix nitrogen and add it to the soil. The dried seed heads are handsome in the winter landscape.

HABIT AND GARDEN USE: Purple prairie clover grows to 1' to 2' high in tight, drooping clumps. Plant has small leaves with three elongated leaflets. Use it toward the front or middle of beds and borders in groups of three to five. Works well in prairies and meadows, and in rock gardens as accent plants.

HOW TO GROW: Plant in moist, humus-rich soil in full sun or light shade. Plants are tough, adaptable and drought tolerant. Clumps seldom need division. Sow seed outdoors in autumn or indoors when ripe. No serious diseases, but rabbits love to mow them down in their prime.

CULTIVARS AND RELATED SPECIES:
D. candida, white prairie clover—Taller, with larger leaves and white flowers; often found in wetter sites, and blooms a week later.

Geranium richardsonii

WILD WHITE GERANIUM

NATIVE HABITAT: Open woods, meadows and prairies in moist soil from the Great Plains west to the Cascades.

HARDINESS ZONE: USDA 4-8, Sunset 3-24

OUTSTANDING FEATURES: This statuesque plant has deeply cut, three- to five-lobed leaves and open clusters of 1" white to pink flowers with rose-pink veins. Plants bloom in early to mid-summer, depending on altitude. The foliage takes on burgundy and purple shades in autumn.

HABIT AND GARDEN USE: Plants form leafy clumps from thick, fibrous-rooted rhizomes. The stout, leafy bloom stalks, to 3' tall, bear open flower clusters in June and July. After blooming, the foliage creates an enchanting groundcover effect. Plant in informal woodland gardens, woods edges, prairies and formal perennial beds, and combine with lupine, iris, gentian, ferns and grasses.

HOW TO GROW: Moist, well-drained humus-rich soil in full sun or partial shade. In time, the creeping rhizomes branch, and can be divided in early spring, after flowering, or in autumn. Self-sown seedlings will appear. No serious pests.

CULTIVARS AND RELATED SPECIES:
G. maculatum, wild geranium—Grows in woods, savannas and prairies in the eastern Great Plains; flower color varies from rose-pink to white.
G. viscosissimum, sticky cranesbill—Similar, but has glandular hairs on the bloom stalk and flowers; grows to 2' tall.

Geranium viscosissimum

PRAIRIE SMOKE

NATIVE HABITAT: Dry to moist gravel or black-soil prairies, savannas and high-mountain meadows from the Canadian tundra south to New York, through the Great Lakes States and across the Plains to the southern Rockies and the Sierras.

HARDINESS ZONE: USDA 1-8, Sunset all zones

OUTSTANDING FEATURES: Furry bloom stalks rise 6" to 12", revealing three 1/2" nodding rose-pink flowers with long purple bracts. Straw-colored petals barely emerge from the end of the tube; the sepals and bracts create the show. The flowers look like miniature serpents rearing their heads. After the flowers fade, the dense heads of feathery, pale rose-pink plumes, or "smoke," for which the plant is so aptly named, appear.

HABIT AND GARDEN USE: Quickly forms a dense groundcover from woody rhizomes. Remove the withered stalks after plumes disperse in May and June. Use

alone or in combination with grasses and low perennials, as in the wild. Choose grasses that emerge early and groundcovers with complementary colors and textures.

HOW TO GROW: Average, well-drained soil in full sun or partial shade. Plants survive climatic extremes, but if you grow them near the edges of their range, procure local stock. Propagate by seed or division. Transplant seedlings when they are 2" to 3" high. Division is faster; lift clumps in early spring or fall.

CULTIVARS AND RELATED SPECIES: *G. rivale,* bog avens—A more open habit, coarser foliage, larger flowers, from dusty pink to white, in open clusters.

Helianthus salicifolius

WILLOW-LEAF SUNFLOWER

NATIVE HABITAT: Dry to moist, calcareous prairies, open woods and savannas from Missouri and Kansas, south to Oklahoma and Texas.

HARDINESS ZONE: USDA 5-9, Sunset all zones

OUTSTANDING FEATURES: Plants form imposing clumps of thin, linear leaves on stalks crowned by 2" bright yellow flowers with purple centers. Tall stems clothed in narrow, lime-green leaves are showy from the time they first emerge in spring.

HABIT AND GARDEN USE: Multi-stemmed crowns form with age to make stout, fibrous-rooted clumps. In full flower, plants may stand 4' or more. The great, fine-textured clumps make pleasing vertical accents in the middle or rear of the garden, and the plant is worth growing for the foliage alone. Combine with grasses, asters, Joe-pye weeds and goldenrods in borders, prairies and meadows.

HOW TO GROW: Dry to moist, well-drained average to rich soil in full sun. Divide clumps in early spring. Take cuttings in early summer. Seed often has low viability, but seedlings will develop quickly. No serious pests.

CULTIVARS AND RELATED SPECIES:
H. maximilianii, Maximilian sunflower—Similar habit but grows to 6', with lanceolate leaves.

BLACKFOOT DAISY

NATIVE HABITAT: Dry, gravelly calcareous soils on prairies, plains and slopes from Kansas and Colorado, south to Texas and Arizona.

HARDINESS ZONE: USDA 7-9, Sunset 1-3, 10-13

OUTSTANDING FEATURES: Rounded clumps of soft gray foliage are covered with 1" yellow-centered white daisies for at least four months. In warmer zones plants may bloom throughout winter as well. Foliage is soft and effective as a foil for other plants.

HABIT AND GARDEN USE: Mature plants form dense, attractive mounds from tough, branched taproots. Set out young plants as established clumps. Use in

beds and borders, informal gardens or in containers; perfect for rock gardens and in the crevices of stone walls with evening primroses, verbenas, phacelias, grasses and cacti.

HOW TO GROW: Average to lean, circumneutral, well-drained soils in full sun. Plants are tough and adaptable, although good drainage is essential or plants will rot. Plant self-sows but is short-lived. No serious pests or diseases.

CULTIVARS AND RELATED SPECIES:
M. cinereum, blackfoot daisy—Very similar; the two species are often placed together.

CENTRAL PRAIRIES & PLAINS

Ratibida pinnata

GRAY-HEADED CONEFLOWER, YELLOW CONEFLOWER

NATIVE HABITAT: Moist, often calcareous black-soil prairies, meadows and woodland edges from Ontario and North Dakota, south to Georgia and Oklahoma; thrives on disturbed ground.

HARDINESS ZONE: USDA 3-8, Sunset all zones

OUTSTANDING FEATURES: Tall, graceful stems sport showy daisy-like flowers with drooping 2" to 3" yellow rays and protruding, egg-shape disks. In autumn the disks turn deep charcoal gray, hence the common name.

HABIT AND GARDEN USE: Multi-stemmed clumps grow 4' to 5' tall on leafy stems from fibrous-rooted crowns. The deep green, pinnately divided leaves have narrow, lobed segments, giving the plant a delicate look. In formal beds and borders, meadows and prairies, adds a windswept look. Combine with grasses, aster, boltonia, ironweed, yarrow and blazing star.

HOW TO GROW: Moist, humus-rich, circumneutral to calcareous soil in full sun or light shade. Plants are easy to establish and grow quickly. Divide overgrown clumps in spring. Self-sown seedlings are numerous. No serious pests.

CULTIVARS AND RELATED SPECIES: *R. columnifera,* Mexican hats— Shorter, to 2-1/2', with short rays, columnar disks and finer-textured foliage.

GIANT BLUE SAGE

NATIVE HABITAT: Dry to moist rocky prairies, woodland edges and clearings, from Missouri and Kansas, south to Oklahoma and Texas. Introduced in the Southeast and western Great Plains.

HARDINESS ZONE: USDA 4-9, Sunset 1-11, 14-24

OUTSTANDING FEATURES: Spikes of deep sky-blue flowers make a lovely show in the late summer and autumn garden. Plants bloom tirelessly for months on end, and foliage is attractive all season.

HABIT AND GARDEN USE: Plants form erect and spreading clumps to 5' or more from fibrous-rooted crowns. The thick, branched stems bear light green, lance-

shaped, toothed leaves, and flower spikes stand above foliage. Perfect for any sunny garden situation, from beds and borders to meadows and prairies. Butterflies and hummingbirds love the flowers. Combine with goldenrods, sunflowers, asters and grasses.

HOW TO GROW: Dry to moist, well-drained, average to rich soil in full sun or light shade. Grows easily from seed or from cuttings taken in summer. Plants are often grown as annuals in colder zones. No serious pests or diseases.

CULTIVARS AND RELATED SPECIES: *S. azurea* var. *grandiflora*—Larger flowers than the typical species. *S. farinacea,* mealy cup sage— Smaller in stature, with deep blue to indigo flowers. Plants are less robust.

Scutellaria resinosa

BUSHY SKULLCAP, RESINOUS SKULLCAP

NATIVE HABITAT: Dry, rocky prairies and high plains from Kansas and Colorado, south to Texas and Arizona.

HARDINESS ZONE: USDA 4-8, Sunset 3-24

OUTSTANDING FEATURES: This short, shrubby plant boasts a profusion of 3/4" deep blue flowers for months in summer. The thick, gray-green oval leaves are decorative when the plant is out of bloom.

HABIT AND GARDEN USE: Many tightly packed stems rise 10" from a woody, tap-rooted crown. Use in rock gardens and the front of beds and borders, as well as informal plantings. Combine with creeping phlox, purple prairie clover, evening primrose, blackfoot daisy, grasses and cacti.

HOW TO GROW: Average to lean, well-drained soil in full sun. Plants thrive on neglect and tolerate all manner of climatic abuse, including cold, heat and wind. Set out young transplants and do not disturb established clumps. Sow seeds in January for transplant by summer. No serious pests or diseases.

CULTIVARS AND RELATED SPECIES: *S. incana,* hoary skullcap—Tall, to 4', with branched terminal clusters of 1" deep blue flowers atop leafy stems.

COMPASS PLANT

NATIVE HABITAT: Dry to moist black-soil prairies from Ohio and Minnesota, south to Alabama and Oklahoma.

HARDINESS ZONE: USDA 4-8, Sunset 3-24

OUTSTANDING FEATURES: Towering stalks bear huge 5" flowers that resemble sunflowers. Narrow rays give flower a refined look despite its size. Huge, deeply lobed leaves form dense, decorative tufts that are impossible for even the most jaded gardener to ignore. Birds, especially goldfinches, give the plant a second tumultuous "bloom" as they vie for the seeds.

HABIT AND GARDEN USE: Shrub-like proportions, large flowers and striking foliage make this an ideal specimen or focal point. Basal rosettes and tall, leafed stalks grow from a huge, branched taproot. Both foliage and flowers show to best advantage in the middle of a border. Place a single plant or small group among lower perennials with fine texture. Combine with yarrow, culver's root, spiderwort, poppy mallow, rattlesnake master and grasses.

HOW TO GROW: Moist, well-drained, humus-rich soil in full sun. Small transplants will quickly grow to elephantine proportions. Plants need plenty of room to spread, so space them 3' to 4' apart. Established clumps are deep rooted and impossible to divide. Sow seeds outdoors in autumn. Self-sown seedlings will appear. No serious pests or diseases.

CULTIVARS AND RELATED SPECIES: *S. perfoliatum,* cup plant—Tall stems pierce the leaf blade, forming an enchanting cup from which birds drink the morning dew. *S. terebinthinaceum,* prairie dock—Huge heart-shaped basal leaves and tall, naked stalks that bear branched clusters of flowers.

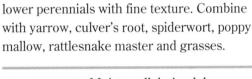

Solidago rigida

STIFF GOLDENROD

NATIVE HABITAT: Dry to moist gravel or black-soil prairies and meadows from Connecticut to Saskatchewan, south to Georgia and New Mexico.

HARDINESS ZONE: USDA Zones 3-9, Sunset all zones

OUTSTANDING FEATURES: An oddity among goldenrods: Flower clusters are large and flattened, creating a showy display of yellow in the late-summer garden. Soft, hairy oval foliage is attractive all season and turns dusty rose in autumn.

HABIT AND GARDEN USE: Erect, multi-stemmed clumps rise 2' to 5' from a basal foliage rosette with a fibrous-rooted crown. Plants are clump-forming, so they are well-behaved garden denizens. Use in beds and borders, meadows and prairies. Combine with asters, mums, yarrow, blazing stars and grasses.

HOW TO GROW: Average to lean, well-drained soil in full sun. Will flop miserably in shade and overly rich soil. Established plants tolerate extremes of heat and cold. Propagate by division in spring or after flowering. Sow seeds in January for transplanting by summer. Self-sown seedlings will appear. No serious pests or diseases.

CULTIVARS AND RELATED SPECIES:
S. speciosa, showy goldenrod—Leafy stems crowned by dense elongated flower clusters; extremely showy in August and September.
S. juncea, early goldenrod—Blooms in August; branched terminal flower clusters resemble yellow fireworks.

HEART-LEAF ALEXANDER

NATIVE HABITAT: Moist to seasonally wet prairies, low meadows, clearings and open woods from New York to British Columbia, south to Georgia and Nevada.

HARDINESS ZONE: USDA 3-8, Sunset all zones

OUTSTANDING FEATURES: Flattened heads of yellow flowers provide a bright accent in the spring garden, when yellow is a welcome color. The lush, heart-shaped leaves are attractive all summer and turn shades of wine in autumn. This parsley relative is a larval food plant for many butterflies, including swallowtails.

HABIT AND GARDEN USE: The open-mounded form of heart-leaf alexander makes it a good weaver for the front or middle of the border. In prairies and meadows, place where it can be appreciated at close range. Combine with columbines, blue phlox and geraniums along woodland walks.

HOW TO GROW: Average to humus-rich, moist soil in full sun to moderate shade. Plants are drought tolerant when established, and form full clumps in a few years' time but seldom require division. Self-sown seedlings will appear. Divide plants in autumn. No serious pests or diseases.

CULTIVARS AND RELATED SPECIES: *Z. aurea,* golden alexander—A bushy plant with many leafy stems. Thrice-divided leaves are more delicate and flower clusters larger.

Anaphalis margaritacea

PEARLY EVERLASTING

NATIVE HABITAT: Meadows, forest openings and rocky slopes from montane to subalpine zones up to 11,000' throughout the western mountains, and along roadsides, burns and clear-cuts in milder climates.

HARDINESS ZONE: USDA 3-8, Sunset 1-9

OUTSTANDING FEATURES: From summer to fall, button-like flowers, which are good for cutting, cover this gray-leaved plant. The white blossoms against the gray-green leaves lighten dull areas and neutralize bold colors. As flowers dry, they continue to provide interest through the winter.

HABIT AND GARDEN USE: Upright, unbranched stems grow 12" to 24" tall. Use in mixed perennial borders, among grasses or woodlands in a naturalized planting or in patio planters. Combine with yarrow, fireweed and penstemon. Flowers retain color and texture when dried, making them excellent for dried bouquets.

HOW TO GROW: Does best in full sun or light shade in well-drained moist soil, although tolerates poor, dry soil. Spreads more rapidly in moist soil. Plant 12" to 15" apart from containers, divisions or seed.

CULTIVARS AND RELATED SPECIES: *A. margaritacea* var. *subalpina*— Smaller, more compact form.

PUSSYTOES, EVERLASTING

NATIVE HABITAT: Gravelly to clay soil with good drainage throughout the Great Plains and eastern base of the Rocky Mountains, and less commonly in western Washington and Nevada.

HARDINESS ZONE: USDA 3-8, Sunset all zones

OUTSTANDING FEATURES: Among the finest of our native groundcovers, pussytoes is noted for its very small matlike rosettes of silver-gray woolly foliage. Tight creamy white to buff spring flower heads resemble cat paws (hence, the common name). Blooms in May for two to three weeks. The evergreen silver foliage adds to winter colors.

HABIT AND GARDEN USE: A ground-hugging plant with leaves that are no more than 6" above ground. Outstanding when grown around edges of sidewalks, between rocks and stone paths or nestled among rocks.

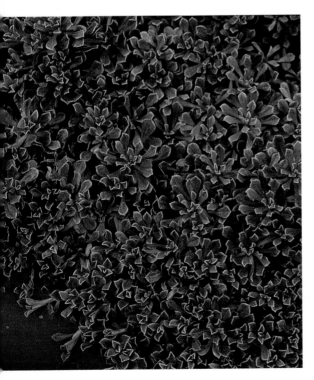

HOW TO GROW: Prefers dry soil; best with 10" to 14" of moisture annually. Tolerates moist soil if well drained. Very drought tolerant; grow in full sun in cool, moist climates or in light, dry shade in hotter, more arid climates. Plant from containers, divisions or by seed in spring to fall.

CULTIVARS AND RELATED SPECIES:
A. rosea—Forms patches of ground-hugging foliage with white to pink flower heads on 2" to 6" upright stems.

Arnica cordifolia

HEART-LEAF ARNICA

NATIVE HABITAT: Ponderosa pine and Douglas-fir forests from 7,000' to 9,000', from Washington to California and eastward to the Rocky Mountains.

HARDINESS ZONE: USDA 4-7, Sunset 2-9

OUTSTANDING FEATURES: Each flowering stem bears one to three radiant, yellow daisy flower heads, a bold contrast to the dark green foliage. An elegant plant, too neat to seem wild. Blooms mid- to late spring or later, depending on elevation and latitude.

HABIT AND GARDEN USE: Spreads by rhizomes but is not vigorous or invasive. Grows 4" to 24" high and may only spread 5" to 8". *Cordifolia* alludes to the basal heart-shaped leaves. Appealing in a mixed perennial border or naturalized among native perennials such as columbine, meadow rue and western blue flag.

HOW TO GROW: Prefers dry shade or moist soil in full sun. Although more commonly found in acid sites, it will grow in neutral to slightly alkaline soil. Plant from containers or seed.

CULTIVARS AND RELATED SPECIES: None.

WESTERN MOUNTAINS & PACIFIC NORTHWEST

CAMASS

NATIVE HABITAT: Moist meadows from British Columbia to California, mostly west of the Cascade mountains and Sierra Nevada.

HARDINESS ZONE: USDA 5-8, Sunset 1-9, 14-17

OUTSTANDING FEATURES: Handsome species growing 2' to 4' tall with upright racemes consisting of star-shaped flowers in shades of purple, blue or white. Blooms for about two weeks, from April to June, depending on environment. Sword-like foliage—1" wide, 2' to 4' tall—makes a striking vertical accent.

Camassia cusickii

HABIT AND GARDEN USE: Combines well with early spring bloomers such as forget-me-nots and pansies, or use as you would tulips or other spring bulbs. Cut flowers for fresh floral display. Clumps expand very slowly.

HOW TO GROW: Plant in fall in average garden loam in full sun or light shade. Tolerates more shade in Rocky Mountain area. Space bulbs 3" to 6" apart, 6" to 8" deep. Keep area moist, especially in spring.

CULTIVARS AND RELATED SPECIES: *C. leichtlinii* 'Alba'—Creamy white flowers.
C. cusickii—Grows on moist hillsides in northeastern Oregon. Dense light blue flowers April to July.
C. quamash—Wider native range from Montana to British Columbia, Utah and California. White or pale blue flowers.

Campanula rotundifolia

COMMON HAREBELL, BLUEBELL

NATIVE HABITAT: Shady, dry mountainsides from foothills to tundra, on rock ledges, in meadows and woods throughout Canada, southward to Nebraska, Colorado and California. Also native to Europe and northern Asia.

HARDINESS ZONE: USDA 3-8, Sunset 1-9, 14-24

OUTSTANDING FEATURES: Delicate, nodding, bell-shaped blue flowers borne on slender stems bloom June to September. Basal foliage is rounded (hence *rotundifolia*). Lower leaves soon disappear, leaving narrow grassy foliage up the stem, which gives the plant an airy appearance.

HABIT AND GARDEN USE: This wonderfully delicate, wiry wildflower grows 6" to 18" tall, 12" to 18" wide. Readily naturalizes in meadow or grassland gardens. Striking when grown in a mixed perennial border or in a woodland setting scattered at the edge of trees or shrubs. Combines especially well with delicate, yellow flowers. Grow with yarrow, pearly everlasting and white flax.

HOW TO GROW: Widely adaptable to moist or dry soils, although it grows more densely in moist, well-drained sites. Transplants easily throughout the growing season from containers, or can be grown from seed.

CULTIVARS AND RELATED SPECIES:
'Flore Pleno'—Blue double flowers.
'Olympica'—Heavy bloomer mid- to late summer, blue flowers.
'Purple Gem'—Purple flowers.
C. rotundifolia var. *alba*—White-flowered form.

Epilobium angustifolium

FIREWEED, WILLOW HERB

NATIVE HABITAT: Montane and subalpine zones throughout most of U.S. and Eurasia, where there has been disturbance such as construction or fire.

HARDINESS ZONE: USDA 3-8, Sunset 1-8

OUTSTANDING FEATURES: Extremely showy rose, magenta or lavender flowers borne on 2-1/2' to 5' stems. Flowers appear from July to September, followed by silky fruits carrying the seeds.

HABIT AND GARDEN USE: Rhizomatous in nature. Needs room to spread and can be invasive. Best naturalized in grassland, meadow or woodland. Combines well with informal shrubs such as species roses or brambles, which mask its rangy look. Bees use nectar to produce flavorful honey.

HOW TO GROW: Flowers best in sun or light shade. Prefers moist soil but tolerates dry soil, where plant is less aggressive. Plant in soils from clay to loams high in organic matter, from containers, division or seed.

CULTIVARS AND RELATED SPECIES:
'Isobel'—Pale pink flowers.
'Album'—White flowers, less aggressive.

Erigeron compositus

CUTLEAF FLEABANE DAISY

NATIVE HABITAT: Rocky, gravelly or sandy areas in open pine forests, mesas and moraines from foothills to subalpine zones, from Washington to California eastward to North and South Dakota and Colorado.

HARDINESS ZONE: USDA 4-7, Sunset 1-7

OUTSTANDING FEATURES: An exceptional wildflower with a refined, neat form, attractive flowers and outstanding foliage. The delicate, dissected, woolly gray leaves orchestrate a background for the white daisy blossoms. Blooms from mid-spring to summer; sometimes, flowers just keep coming.

HABIT AND GARDEN USE: A dwarf daisy 3" to 10" tall, 6" to 12" wide. Superior for rock gardens, edges, troughs or containers.

HOW TO GROW: Adaptable to most soils as long as they drain well. Grows well in alkaline (pH 8) sandy loam; spreads more slowly in clay. Plant in dry soil in full sun or partial shade. Plant from containers or seed.

CULTIVARS AND RELATED SPECIES:
'Albus'—Snow-white flowers.
E. compositus var. *glabratus*—Leaves less dissected, white flowers.

Eriogonum umbellatum

SULFUR FLOWER, WESTERN MOUNTAIN BUCKWHEAT

NATIVE HABITAT: Open woods and meadows, rocky outcrops and dry valleys, grasslands and mesas, from Wyoming to Colorado to California and Washington.

HARDINESS ZONE: USDA 3-8, Sunset all zones

OUTSTANDING FEATURES: One of the finest native perennials for spectacular flowers and foliage. A four-season plant: The sulfur-yellow flower heads open in spring and extend into summer; as they age, they transform into shades of orange and red, providing good winter color. White hairs often cover the underside of the dark green leaves. In fall, the leaves turn red and purple to brown.

HABIT AND GARDEN USE: Erect or prostrate and slightly spreading, sulfur flower usually forms a mat but can be a subshrub. Generally 6" to 12" tall, 8" to 12" wide. Superior in rock gardens, creeping between crevices or dangling over rock walls. Flowers picked before they mature retain their brilliant color, making excellent pressed specimens and dried bouquets.

HOW TO GROW: Prefers full sun to light shade in loose, gravelly soil. A dryland species, it will grow in amended or unamended soil as long as it drains well. Best planted in spring from containers or seed.

CULTIVARS AND RELATED SPECIES:
E. umbellatum var. *porterii* ('Porterii')—Dense, compact form, yellow flowers.
E. umbellatum var. *subalpinum*—Creamy white flowers maturing to pink.
E. umbellatum var. *torreyanum*—Dark green foliage, not woolly; yellow flowers.

WESTERN MOUNTAINS & PACIFIC NORTHWEST

Iris missouriensis

WESTERN BLUE FLAG, WILD IRIS

NATIVE HABITAT: Meadows and streambanks from North Dakota to Washington, southward to Colorado and Nevada, in areas flooded with snow water or in catch basins of low rainfall areas.

HARDINESS ZONE: USDA 4-7, Sunset 1-10

OUTSTANDING FEATURES: Unrivaled for its noble look and its narrow blue-green foliage, this is a standout among plants. Usually forms two flowers per stem, which are generally pale blue, but may be violet or white. Blooms from May to July, depending on latitude and elevation.

HABIT AND GARDEN USE: This narrow plant, 1' to 1-1/2' wide and 2' tall, is easily naturalized in meadow gardens or mixed perennial borders.

HOW TO GROW: Thrives in open spaces and full sun with adequate moisture, especially in spring. Prefers drier soil during summer. Plant from container, seed or rhizome. Mix with columbines, *Thermopsis montana,* meadow rue, geraniums and *Achillea lanulosa.*

CULTIVARS AND RELATED SPECIES:
'Alba'—White flowers.

Linum perenne ssp. *lewisii (Linum lewisii)*

WILD BLUE FLAX

NATIVE HABITAT: Plains to high ridges as well as mid-elevation mountain meadows of western North America.

HARDINESS ZONE: USDA 3-8, Sunset all zones

OUTSTANDING FEATURES: Delicate blue, saucer-shaped flowers borne on slender wiry stems, profuse blooms from May into summer. Flowers open early morning and fall by midday in the hot sun. Makes poor cut flower, as petals detach readily.

HABIT AND GARDEN USE: A noteworthy wildflower 4" to 30" tall and 12" to 18" across. Its airiness lends itself to a variety of settings—rock gardens, mixed perennial borders, along the edge of water pools and scattered among grasses in prairie or meadow plantings. Combine with other delicate flowers in pink shades or yellow, such as *Thermopsis* spp.

HOW TO GROW: Prefers lean soils. Adaptable to dry or moist soils in sun or partial shade. Transplants easily from containers any time, or grows freely from seed.

CULTIVARS AND RELATED SPECIES:
L.p. 'Alba'—White flowers.
L.p. 'Saphir' ('Sapphire')—Dwarf form 12" by 12", sapphire blue flowers.

BLUE MIST PENSTEMON

NATIVE HABITAT: Rocky slopes and open woods of ponderosa pine forest, on north-facing cliffs and mesas; from southeast Wyoming to southern Colorado.

HARDINESS ZONE: USDA 4-7, Sunset 1-7

OUTSTANDING FEATURES: A mist of flowers resting on slender erect stems 8" to 12" high in June and July against a background of dark, glossy green delicate foliage. Flowers are blue to blue-violet and about 1/2" long. A long-lived perennial.

HABIT AND GARDEN USE: This nonaggressive, well-behaved wildflower combines well with sulfur flower and cutleaf fleabane daisy. Effective in group plantings, rock gardens or mixed perennial borders.

HOW TO GROW: Grow in full sun or light, dry shade. Not tolerant of too much winter moisture around the crown. Crushed stone makes a better mulch than wood or bark. Prefers acid soil but tolerant of neutral to slightly alkaline sites.

CULTIVARS AND RELATED SPECIES:
White and pink flower forms in the wild.

GOLDEN BANNER, FALSE LUPINE

NATIVE HABITAT: Wet meadows and well-drained sites from Washington to Montana, south to Colorado and Nevada.

HARDINESS ZONE: USDA 4-8, Sunset 1-9

OUTSTANDING FEATURES: Tall racemes of vivid yellow flowers 6" to 8" long. Blooms several weeks from late spring to mid-summer. Flowers are slightly fragrant and persist for several weeks.

HABIT AND GARDEN USE: This midsize plant grows to 2' to 3' tall, and has a rhizomatous nature, so it can be invasive. Combines well with wild iris and harebell. Excellent for fresh floral arrangements.

HOW TO GROW: Easily planted from container or grown from seed. Difficult to transplant once established. Best in full sun to partial shade in moist, fertile soil.

CULTIVARS AND RELATED SPECIES:
T. rhombifolia—East of Rocky Mountains, earlier bloomer.

Berlandiera lyrata

CHOCOLATE FLOWER

NATIVE HABITAT: Roadsides and basins in high desert grasslands from 4,000' to 7,000'. Most prolific in brilliantly sunny places where runoff collects.

HARDINESS ZONE: USDA 4b-8, as long as soil stays moderately dry while cold, Sunset 3-24

OUTSTANDING FEATURES: Both the rosettes of pale green leaves and the yellow daisies borne on foot-tall stems from early spring throughout the summer have a subtle chocolaty aroma, most pungent in the cool morning and night air. Green cup-like seed receptacles replace the faded flowers and make interesting additions to dried bouquets.

HABIT AND GARDEN USE: Chocolate flower quickly develops a thick, fleshy taproot that stores moisture efficiently between waterings. Plants are long-lived and also easily grown from seed with no pre-treatment, any time the soil is warm. Flowers droop in midday heat, so group with other colorful wildflowers—desert and bush penstemon, blackfoot daisy and fern verbena.

HOW TO GROW: One of the most heat- and drought-tolerant desert flowers, chocolate flower prefers well-drained sandy or gravelly soil lacking organic matter. Deep watering every two weeks during the growing season keeps it constantly in bloom. Established plants should not be disturbed and seedlings transplant best while young, before deep roots anchor it in place.

CULTIVARS AND RELATED SPECIES: None.

WINECUPS, POPPY MALLOW

NATIVE HABITAT: High desert and prairie grasslands below 6,500' receiving at least 12" of rainfall annually, where plants form small colonies in deep sandy soils.

HARDINESS ZONE: USDA 4b-8, Sunset all zones

OUTSTANDING FEATURES: In late spring through summer, wine-red flowers 2" in diameter seem to glow in the sunlight, floating at the ends of slender upturned stems that sprawl along the ground from a rosette of rounded, lobed leaves.

HABIT AND GARDEN USE: Low-spreading form and long bloom season make winecups a lovely groundcover, a graceful accent between boulders in a rock garden or along a dry streambed or garden path—especially combined with a silver-leafed color foil such as silver-spreader artemisia or woolly thyme. Winecups

also add an elegant note planted in drifts in mown and unmown buffalograss.

HOW TO GROW: Unlike many dryland plants, winecups will grow well in organically amended soil, though it is not necessary for plants to thrive. Thick fleshy roots extend deep into well-drained, porous soil, and deep summer watering every one to two weeks keeps plants from lapsing into dormancy. Winecups can be propagated by root segments as well as by seeds, which germinate slowly and erratically.

CULTIVARS AND RELATED SPECIES: None.

Calylophus hartwegii

SUNDROPS

NATIVE HABITAT: Short prairie grasses and rocky foothill slopes to 8,000', where at least 12" of rain falls annually.

HARDINESS ZONE: USDA 5a-8, Sunset 1-3, 10-13

OUTSTANDING FEATURES: A mass of wiry stems densely covered with narrow green leaves and an abundance of yellow blossoms provide a feeling of lushness on a modest water budget. Like related evening primroses, bright yellow flowers open in the cool evening hours and fade to salmon pink by the following midday.

HABIT AND GARDEN USE: Sundrops can be massed, planted 12" to 18" apart as a colorful groundcover or planted among boulders to stabilize soil on slopes. Mix with fern verbena, cherry sage or Russian sage for contrast in beds and borders.

HOW TO GROW: Unparticular about soil, sundrops' pithy, much-branched roots adapt to loose sandy or gravelly soils or heavier clay loam as long as it is not too wet. Increase plants by division in spring. In nature, plants flower heavily in spring and again in response to summer rains, but sundrops can be kept in continuous bloom by deep watering every one to two weeks through summer.

CULTIVARS AND RELATED SPECIES: *C. serrulatus*—Very similar, with slightly smaller flowers. Also similar to white-tufted and Mexican evening primroses, gaura and hummingbird trumpet *(Epilobium canum* ssp. *canum,* formerly known as *Zauschneria).*

GAURA

NATIVE HABITAT: Low-lying basins along floodplains below 4,000' in sun-baked south Texas.

HARDINESS ZONE: USDA 5b-9, Sunset all zones

OUTSTANDING FEATURES: From a modest rosette of narrow leaves, 2'-tall fountains of delicate flowers, with four petals held upward and eight long stamens swept downward, appear in flushes from late spring to early autumn. Masses of white flowers suffused with pink along with the wiry dark green stems and leaves spotted red make gaura an elegant addition to flower beds and borders.

HABIT AND GARDEN USE: Planted in drifts with perennials such as blue flax, penstemon, purple coneflower, pitcher sage, gaillardia and Russian sage, gaura

enhances its companions in the middle ground of borders. Trim off spent flower stems occasionally to limit self-sowing or trim back after frost to tidy the garden for winter.

HOW TO GROW: Though adapted to periodic deluges that interrupt the hot, dry summer, plants growing in full sun in sandy loam soil and watered deeply every week will bloom continuously. In heavier soil or partial shade, water less. The trade-off for such profusion is a shorter life span: Plants exhaust themselves after several summers. Gaura is easily grown from volunteer seedlings transplanted in early spring or fall.

CULTIVARS AND RELATED SPECIES: *G. coccinea,* scarlet gaura—Shorter stems and smaller pink flowers; rarely cultivated but enjoyed for its color and sweet fragrance where it grows wild.

Hymenoxys scaposa

PERKY SUE

NATIVE HABITAT: High plains, shortgrass prairie from southern Kansas to Colorado, south to Texas and New Mexico, dotting dry rocky slopes and rolling hills below 7,500'.

HARDINESS ZONE: USDA 4b-8, Sunset 1-3, 10-13

OUTSTANDING FEATURES: Small rosettes of narrow silky silver leaves support a continuing display of yellow daisies on short wiry stems from April to October. Over time, older plants often branch from the thick taproot, forming self-contained little colonies, but individual plants are long-lived and require no dividing or trimming to remain neat and colorful.

HABIT AND GARDEN USE: Use to border flower beds and paths, grow between boulders in rock gardens and interplant with mat or pineleaf penstemon, scarlet globemallow, flameflower or the low-spreading veronicas, for contrast.

HOW TO GROW: Seeds germinate easily when freshly harvested. The offsets of older plants can be transplanted in early spring. Plants prefer fine stone or scree mulches to bark or other organic mulches and are very long-lived in poor, unimproved soils. Perfect for the most casual gardeners.

CULTIVARS AND RELATED SPECIES:
H. acaulis, stemless perky Sue—Flowers nestle in tufts of silver leaves; plant between flagstones or stepping stones.

GIANT FOUR O'CLOCK

NATIVE HABITAT: Plains in pinyon, juniper and oak woodlands below 7,500' from west Texas through New Mexico and Arizona, in well-drained soils receiving winter rain or snow.

HARDINESS ZONE: USDA 5a-8, Sunset 4-24

OUTSTANDING FEATURES: Lush-looking, with thick, light green, heart-shaped leaves and a profusion of magenta trumpet flowers that open late in the afternoon and close again the following morning. In full sun with deep bi-weekly summer watering, it grows as a dense mound 18" high and 2' to 3' in diameter. With more water and less light, a single plant may sprawl across 8' of space or cascade over banks and low retaining walls.

HABIT AND GARDEN USE: Use as an accent shrub or groundcover for color from May to September. In autumn, the entire top growth dies back and detaches cleanly from the deep, 4"-diameter root (which makes established plants difficult to eliminate). Interplant with evergreens to balance the dormant season void. Its primary pollinator is the large sphinx moth or hummingbird moth, whose evening nectar-sipping activity is a treat to watch but whose larvae, tomato hornworms, are a vegetable garden pest.

HOW TO GROW: Well-drained soil is essential since, if too wet, the fleshy root will rot. Young plants (one to two years old) transplant easily any time from containers, or just as they begin to emerge. Deep summer watering once or twice monthly is all the encouragement needed.

CULTIVARS AND RELATED SPECIES: *M. jalapa* 'Marvel of Peru', old-fashioned four o'clock—Annual in colder areas but perennial in the south and warm desert west, grows to 3' to 4' and equally wide with yellow or rose-pink flowers and reseeds prolifically.

Oenothera caespitosa

WHITE-TUFTED EVENING PRIMROSE

NATIVE HABITAT: Sunny slopes and grassy plains below 7,500' throughout the intermountain West, where as little as 8" of rain falls.

HARDINESS ZONE: USDA 4b-8, Sunset 1-3, 7-14, 18-21

OUTSTANDING FEATURES: Produces a bouquet of silken white cup-shaped flowers, each growing up to 4" in diameter, within a dense mound of long, narrow, velvety leaves. An extensive fleshy root system makes plants heat- and drought-tolerant and long-lived.

HABIT AND GARDEN USE: Plants grow best in well-drained gritty sand or decomposed granite soils with no organic amendments, in full sun or partial shade. Compact mounds vary from 12" to 24" across and 6" to 12" high, depending on the availability of sunlight and water. With deep bi-weekly watering, plants will flower from early spring to autumn. Use in rock gardens, to edge borders or paths or combine them in beds with fern verbena, paperflower, pentemons, globemallow and other drought-adapted wildflowers.

HOW TO GROW: Container-grown plants transplant well any time but water sparingly during cool weather. Plants require no division and are best left undisturbed except for trimming spent leaves and seedpods occasionally.

CULTIVARS AND RELATED SPECIES: *O. berlandiera,* Mexican evening primrose—Darker pink flowers remain open throughout the day. *O. speciosa,* showy evening primrose—Pale pink to white blossoms open late in the afternoon and fade in the heat of the following morning.

PINK PLAINS PENSTEMON

NATIVE HABITAT: The plains of Kansas to California and south to Mexico, sharing moisture with grasses of the Great Plains and periodically colonizing flooded arroyos in drier southern deserts.

HARDINESS ZONE: USDA 4b-9, Sunset 7-15, 18-21

OUTSTANDING FEATURES: Does best in spaces too hot and dry for other perennials, and balances its dense growth of wiry stems with a network of pith-sheathed roots that extend 6' and deeper into sandy or rocky soils. In May, and after summer rains in September, plants are smothered in delicate lavender-pink flowers.

HABIT AND GARDEN USE: A subshrub forming compact mounds 2' tall and wide. Lean, well-drained soil and intense sunlight are essential for vigorous plants and billowy masses of flowers. Combine with desert shrubs—Apache plume, cliffrose and creosote bush; penstemon's pale flowers contrast with the dark green foliage. Blackfoot daisy, white-tufted evening primrose, globemallow, chocolate flower and desert zinnia are good companions in flower beds.

HOW TO GROW: Young, container-grown plants transplant best in warm weather; bush penstemon is especially sensitive to overwatering while dormant. Penstemon prefers fine gravel mulch or no mulch rather than organic mulches, which promote crown rot.

CULTIVARS AND RELATED SPECIES:
There are more than 200 species of penstemon native throughout the U.S., particularly the West.
P. pseudospectabilis, desert beardtongue—Large herbaceous species with basal rosette of stiff, leathery dark blue-green evergreen foliage and deep rose-pink flowers, which attract hummingbirds.

WESTERN DESERTS

Salvia greggii

CHERRY SAGE, AUTUMN SAGE

NATIVE HABITAT: Rocky slopes and canyons below 8,000' in south central and southwest Texas and adjacent Mexico.

HARDINESS ZONE: USDA 5b/6a-10, Sunset 8-24

OUTSTANDING FEATURES: A long season of color, and nectar for hummingbirds on their northern sojourn. Single plants are large enough, with blooms bright and profuse enough, to have impact in small gardens. Species is rose-pink.

HABIT AND GARDEN USE: Plant forms a small, densely twiggy mound to 2' tall and a bit wider, with small oblong leaves and spikes of tubular flowers, April to November. Tuck in between masses of evergreen cotoneasters or interplant with English lavender, curry plant or santolina as low maintenance groundcovers in larger gardens. The hotter the microclimate, the more cherry sage benefits from filtered shade.

HOW TO GROW: Where plant is marginally cold hardy, minimize winter damage by planting in late spring, and prune established plants at that time, removing old growth back to new leaves. Mulch well to insulate roots from heat and cold and conserve soil moisture. In warmer areas, trim plants occasionally to keep them compact. Deep bi-weekly watering when plants are actively growing, and monthly while dormant, keeps them vigorous. Young volunteer seedlings transplant easily in spring, and new plants can also be grown from semi-woody cuttings.

CULTIVARS AND RELATED SPECIES:
'Cardinal Red'—Rich red; other unnamed selections include coral pink, purple and white.
S. pinquefolia, rock sage—Native to desert foothills, reaches 4' tall and 2' wide with wine-colored flowers.
S. dorrii, desert sage—Compact silver-leaved evergreen mound with blue flower spikes, grows to 1' tall and 2' wide.

Talinum calycinum

FLAMEFLOWER

NATIVE HABITAT: High plains grasslands below 7,500' from Nebraska west to Colorado and south into Texas.

HARDINESS ZONE: USDA 5a, Sunset 2-18

OUTSTANDING FEATURES: If you didn't know its native range, you'd think flameflower an alpine species. Its succulent linear green leaves form tufts up to 6" high and wide from a small, fleshy underground stem. Each afternoon from early summer to frost, the plant produces a profusion of magenta flowers nearly an inch in diameter that float 8" above the clumps of leaves on wiry gold stems.

HABIT AND GARDEN USE: Plant in rock gardens or in beds with deeply rooted perennials such as Wasatch or mat penstemon, artemisias such as Roman wormwood, silver spreader or pussytoes, creeping baby's breath, desert zinnia or the native fringed sage. Plant for drifts of color in unmown buffalograss. Flameflower can often get by with watering twice a month while flowering.

HOW TO GROW: Individual plants survive many years and reseed vigorously in

loose gritty soil. Flameflower overwinters with only a small tuber-like underground stem regrowing new roots each year, so soil should be well drained or fairly dry in winter to avoid rot. Seedlings transplant easily before flowering begins. New plants are also easily grown from disbudded stem cuttings in summer.

CULTIVARS AND RELATED SPECIES:
None are commercially available.

Verbena (Glandularia) bipinnatifida

FERN VERBENA, PRAIRIE VERVAIN

NATIVE HABITAT: Gravelly slopes, roadsides and sparse grasslands from 5,000' to 10,000' from South Dakota south to Mexico, and from Alabama west to Arizona.

HARDINESS ZONE: USDA 4-8, Sunset all zones

OUTSTANDING FEATURES: One of the first wildflowers to brighten the rocky desert foothills, fern verbena has wiry stems less than 1' high that spread 18" wide, and finely divided foliage. Lavender-purple umbels of flowers appear in early spring, stop in summer's heat and often appear again with late summer rains.

HABIT AND GARDEN USE: Showy when blooming, inconspicuous when not, fern verbena is an excellent filler for rock gardens, beds and bordering paths. Blend with white-tufted evening primrose, perky Sue, blackfoot daisy, sundrops and the dryland and foothills penstemons. Short-lived in nature, fern verbena reseeds well in gravelly or sandy soils. Remove spent plants and relocate misplaced volunteers in spring, or enjoy their surprise appearance in a more casual garden.

HOW TO GROW: Most easily started from small container-grown plants. Disbudded semi-soft stem cuttings root easily in summer. Trim established plants after flowering or leave them to reseed and increase.

CULTIVARS AND RELATED SPECIES:

V. gooddingii, desert verbena—Adapted to warmer low-desert conditions, and flowers are pink.
V. tenuisecta (G. pulchella), moss verbena—Annual in Zone 5 and colder climates; flowers through summer.
V. canadensis, clump verbena—A high-plains native with magenta flowers; longer-lived in colder climates.

DESERT ZINNIA, PRAIRIE ZINNIA, ROCKY MOUNTAIN ZINNIA

NATIVE HABITAT: From the plains of Kansas to the foothills of the Rockies south into Mexico, between 3,000' and 7,000'.

HARDINESS ZONE: USDA 5-9, Sunset all zones

OUTSTANDING FEATURES: Depending on the soil and moisture available, desert zinnia forms colonies of individual tufted plants or solid carpets of groundcover. Stems are 4" high, wiry and pale green with fine needle-like leaves to the tips where 1"-diameter, papery yellow daisies with broad rays bloom from May to October. When not in flower, plants look like tufts of fine grass.

HABIT AND GARDEN USE: Desert zinnia is long-lived and non-invasive and spreads by a network of wiry rhizomatous roots 1' below the soil surface. A very undemanding groundcover for dry rock gardens, between flagstones in paths and sunny patios, and as a border for beds of equally drought-hardy wildflowers—blackfoot daisy, penstemons, verbena, flameflower, purple groundcherry, globemallow and gayfeather.

HOW TO GROW: For fast coverage, space small container-grown plants 8" to 10" apart when soil is warm. Established plantings can be mowed late in winter as a cleanup. Seeds germinate erratically at best, preferring warm, well-drained soil

kept moderately damp to start. Deep watering once or twice a month in summer keeps plants blooming.

CULTIVARS AND RELATED SPECIES:
Z. acerosa, white desert zinnia—Very similar in form, with smaller white flowers; native only in the southern deserts.

Armeria maritima var. *californica*

THRIFT, SEA PINK

NATIVE HABITAT: Sandy soils or well-drained slopes on sand dunes, coastal grasslands, bluffs and ridges from central to northern California.

HARDINESS ZONE: USDA 6-10, Sunset all zones

OUTSTANDING FEATURES: A low, ground-hugging plant with tidy, fine-textured foliage and distinctive pink, ball-shaped flowers. Blooms year-round in coastal gardens, with the greatest profusion in mid-spring. A petite, handsome grass-like plant, highly popular for use in pots, rock gardens and along the front of borders.

HABIT AND GARDEN USE: This mounding species reaches 6" to 8" tall and 10" to 12" across. Plants slowly spread by rhizomes to form a dense carpet-like mat. Delightful in meandering drifts along walls and walks, as well as in geometrical planting patterns and as a groundcover, with native dudleyas, wallflower and paintbrush.

HOW TO GROW: Plant in late fall through early spring from containers or divisions in sunny locations. Requires good drainage and performs best with regular watering, particularly when planted in warmer and drier inland zones. Its long flowering season and good appearance can be extended by removing spent flower heads every one to two weeks.

CULTIVARS AND RELATED SPECIES: *A. maritima*—Widely distributed, with many subtle foliage and flowering variations found in the trade, depending upon geographical location.

CALIFORNIA

COASTAL SAGEWORT

NATIVE HABITAT: Coastal strand plant communities from central California into Oregon in rocky and sandy soils on dunes and bluffs.

HARDINESS ZONE: USDA 9-10, Sunset 4, 5, 7-9, 14-24

OUTSTANDING FEATURES: This perennial immediately captures the eye because of its soft texture and gray-green foliage. Its finely divided leaves create a sense of delicacy and refinement, and invite touch.

HABIT AND GARDEN USE: A low-spreading plant, growing 12" to 18" high, 18" to 24" across. Tiny, insignificant flowers occur on numerous, highly visible spike-like inflorescences. A good plant for banks and rock gardens in small spaces, particularly around patios and seating areas, with seaside daisies, dudleyas and sea lavenders.

Artemisia pycnocephala 'David's Choice'

HOW TO GROW: Plant from containers, preferably in late fall. Water regularly until winter rains begin. In coastal regions, plants need only periodic summer water, if any; in hotter inland gardens, plants prefer bi-weekly watering. Plant does best with good drainage and removal of spent flower spikes. Replace every two to four years.

CULTIVARS AND RELATED SPECIES: 'David's Choice'—Denser foliage habit and tighter clusters of flower spikes, 10" to 12" tall.

CALIFORNIA

Camissonia cheiranthifolia

BEACH EVENING PRIMROSE

NATIVE HABITAT: Coastal strand plant communities from southern Oregon to Baja California on sandy sites such as dunes and flats.

HARDINESS ZONE: USDA 9-10, Sunset 14-17, 19-24

OUTSTANDING FEATURES: Clear yellow flowers, gray-green foliage and very low spreading habit make this an ideal plant for naturalizing and soil stabilization on slopes in coastal gardens and for scrambling over rocks. Its abundant flowering provides a long season of summer color.

HABIT AND GARDEN USE: A low-growing perennial with a taproot, reaching 6" to 8 high, 2' to 3' in diameter. Leaves are pale gray-green, and sometimes covered with fine hairs. Good flowering accent in small garden spaces.

HOW TO GROW: Plant from container or seed in mid- to late fall. Plants are short-lived—they last only two to three years—but reseed readily and grow rapidly to provide an ongoing source of new plants. Needs well-drained soils and only monthly summer watering in coastal gardens; bi-monthly drip irrigation in drier inland locations. Trim unwanted stems after flowering is complete in late summer.

CULTIVARS AND RELATED SPECIES:
Numerous western native species, many from desert habitats, are available as seed from local sources, including, *C. californica*, *C. campestris* and *C. cardiophylla*. (Plants now classified as *Camissonia* until recently were included in the genus *Oenothera*.)

CHALK DUDLEYA

NATIVE HABITAT: Cliffs and rocky coastal areas from central California to northern Baja California.

HARDINESS ZONE: USDA 9-10, Sunset 2, 3, 7,10-24

OUTSTANDING FEATURES: This large succulent produces a 1' to 2' diameter rosette of striking, ghostly gray-white foliage, enhanced by several 2' to 3' tall flower stalks each spring. A marvelous container and rock-garden specimen plant.

HABIT AND GARDEN USE: This low-growing succulent is the giant of its genus. Broad, lance-shaped leaves are covered with powder and wax, producing a distinctive color, and curve upward, ending in a pointed tip. Numerous small red flowers are noticeable when viewed closely. Use as a specimen element, singly

or in small groups in raised planters, on banks and in specialty succulent gardens.

HOW TO GROW: Plant from divisions or containers in late spring to early summer. Water sparingly until new growth is apparent; established plants seldom need summer water. Plant in light, well-draining soils, in full sun. An easy garden plant as long as you avoid heavy soils and over-watering.

CULTIVARS AND RELATED SPECIES: Hardier subspecies, found in the desert mountains of Arizona and Nevada, are grown locally for ornamental gardens.
D. cymosa—Noted for its bright red-orange flowers.
D. farinosa, bluff lettuce—Light yellow flowers and red-tipped green leaves.

CALIFORNIA

Epilobium canum ssp. *canum (Zauschneria californica)*

CALIFORNIA FUCHSIA

NATIVE HABITAT: Common on dry slopes and ridges below 10,000' throughout the West and northern Mexico.

HARDINESS ZONE: USDA 9-10, Sunset 2-10, 12-24

OUTSTANDING FEATURES: A striking combination of soft gray-green foliage and intensive red-orange tubular flowers, stunning during summer-fall peak when most dry climate plants are dormant. Well loved for its nectar, particularly by hummingbirds.

HABIT AND GARDEN USE: A mounding to spreading plant with an open habit, reaching 12" to 18" high, 3' to 4' across. Narrow gray-green leaves produce a soft texture. An important plant for both color and wildlife interest. Excellent in mixed borders and on slopes with species from the sage-scrub and chaparral plant communities such as mimulus, penstemon and dudleyas.

HOW TO GROW: Establish from seed or containers in late fall before winter rains. Select sunny locations with light soils or fast-draining conditions for best performance. Allow plants to flower late into fall and produce seed; trim lightly in winter or early spring, when foliage is sparse, to control shape and size.

CULTIVARS AND RELATED SPECIES: *E. canum*—The species is particularly drought-tolerant and easy to hybridize. *E. canum* ssp. *latifolium* 'Solidarity Pink'—Soft pink flower color.

SEASIDE DAISY

NATIVE HABITAT: Coastal bluffs and sand dunes from Oregon to central and southern California.

HARDINESS ZONE: USDA 9-10, Sunset 14-24

OUTSTANDING FEATURES: A very reliable garden plant for both coastal and inland gardens, with a neat mounding habit and handsome medium green foliage. Large daisy-type flowers occur from late spring through summer, and through fall in coastal zones.

HABIT AND GARDEN USE: Low-growing perennial, 10" to 12" tall, 2' to 3' across. Eye-catching, 2"-diameter flowers have purple-blue rays and yellow centers. Well suited for use among rocks, on banks and in casual drifts along meandering pathways, with sea lavender, dudleyas, sedums and echeverias.

HOW TO GROW: Plant from seed, containers or divisions in late fall to establish during the moist winter season. Prefers well-drained soils with weekly watering

through the warm summer months to sustain optimal foliage quality. Flowers best in full sun in coastal regions; avoid planting in intense afternoon sun in inland gardens.

CULTIVARS AND RELATED SPECIES:
'Cape Sebastian'—Compact, ground-hugging, with smaller flowers and tighter foliage habit.
Western natives *E. cervinus* (Siskiyou daisy) and *E. compositus* (alpine daisy) show good garden tolerance.

Eschscholzia californica var. *maritima*

CALIFORNIA POPPY

NATIVE HABITAT: Coastal dunes, slopes and bluffs from central to northern California.

HARDINESS ZONE: USDA 9-10, Sunset 4,5, 7-9, 14-24

OUTSTANDING FEATURES: California's state flower is characterized by intense golden-orange flowers and pale green, finely textured foliage. Excels as a perennial in the coastal zones and inland with its spreading habit and two-month-long flowering cycle in late spring and early summer.

HABIT AND GARDEN USE: A fast-growing perennial that develops a woody stem and spreading habit, maturing 10" to 18" high, 24" to 30" across. Soft, finely divided herbaceous leaves occur mainly from the base of the plant. Well suited as a flowering accent in mixed natural plantings on slopes, bluffs and in wildflower gardens.

HOW TO GROW: In late fall, sow seed in sandy or other well-drained soils in full sun. Seeds germinate during winter rains and flower in their first season. In warmer inland gardens, periodic drip irrigation can extend the flowering season. Allow flower heads to mature to produce new crop of seeds; trim in late fall to manage size and renew foliage. Replace older plants every three to five years. Can be used as a mass wildflower planting or in combination with blue-eyed grass, clarkia and lupine.

CULTIVARS AND RELATED SPECIES:
E. californica—Annual and perennial, widely adapted. Flowers vary from pale yellow to deep orange.
E. minutiflora—Desert species with yellow flowers.

SOUTHERN BUSH MONKEY FLOWER

NATIVE HABITAT: Coastal sage scrub and chaparral plant communities on steep cliff faces, disturbed slopes, dry foothills and plains.

HARDINESS ZONE: USDA 9-10, Sunset 7-9, 14-24

OUTSTANDING FEATURES: Distinctive, funnel-shaped flowers occur in large numbers from mid-spring into summer. One of the best flowering accent plants for summer value in dry-climate gardens.

HABIT AND GARDEN USE: A mounding to sprawling species developing herbaceous seasonal growth and older woody stems. Typically grows 2' to 3' tall, spreading 2' to 4' across. Medium to deep green leaves are narrow and long, creating an attractive backdrop while flowering. Good nectar value for wildlife and in combination with salvias, penstemons and wild lilacs.

HOW TO GROW: Plant from containers or seed in late fall, in sunny locations and well-drained soils. Water weekly until onset of winter rains. Requires little or no supplemental water after the first winter, but will grow larger, with lusher

foliage, with bi-monthly drip irrigation. Under drought stress, plant sheds leaves, resulting in a sparse appearance. Trim plant in late fall to remove water-stressed stems and foliage.

CULTIVARS AND RELATED SPECIES:
M. 'Verity Hybrids'—Short-lived group with profuse clusters of large red, purple, cream, white or yellow flowers on compact, bush-like plants.

CALIFORNIA

Penstemon centranthifolius

SCARLET BUGLER

NATIVE HABITAT: Dry openings and bare spots in oak woodland and chaparral throughout California, below 5,000'.

HARDINESS ZONE: USDA 9-10, Sunset 7-23

OUTSTANDING FEATURES: A striking color accent plant with upright branching habit, distinctive gray-green foliage and richly contrasting intense red flowers on tall stems to 5'. Provides high-impact visual character individually or in groupings.

HABIT AND GARDEN USE: This semi-woody perennial develops basal branches for both foliage and flowers. Leaves grow 1" to 3" long; plants, 1' to 3' high. A marvelous accent on slopes, in raised planters and mixed among other native shrubs and perennials in natural gardens. Good nectar value for wildlife.

HOW TO GROW: Plant from containers or seed in fall for best results, in sunny location in loose, fast-draining soil. Water weekly until winter rains begin. Established plants need little or no summer water. Allow flowers to mature for seeds, and remove stalks at the end of summer. Most plants need to be replaced every three to four years.

CULTIVARS AND RELATED SPECIES:
P. spectabilis, royal penstemon—Blue-purple flowers; 2' to 4' tall.
P. heterophyllus, foothill penste-mon—Spreads 2' to 3' across, 12" to 15" tall, and has deep purple flowers
P. superbus—Gray-green foliage and bright red flowers on 3' to 4' stalks.

MATILIJA POPPY

NATIVE HABITAT: Inland and foothill areas of southern California, in dry washes and canyons with seasonal runoff from winter rains.

HARDINESS ZONE: USDA 9-10, Sunset all zones

OUTSTANDING FEATURES: Magnificent flowers—the largest of any California native—grow 5" to 7" across, with six large white petals clustered around a 1" sphere of intense yellow stamens. Flowers are produced in profusion in late spring to mid-summer.

HABIT AND GARDEN USE: This remarkably robust plant develops numerous upright stems from aggressive underground rhizomes. Plants often reach 6' to 8' tall and can spread many feet across. Distinctive gray foliage is deeply cut with pointed lobes. One of the most striking accent plants for dry gardens. Needs ample space and careful management.

HOW TO GROW: Plant from containers in late fall in sunny location with well-drained soil. Be advised that this plant spreads aggressively and requires yearly digging to remove migrating rhizomes. Each winter its new stems quickly reach their full height and put out flower buds. Allow plants to complete flowering and to stand until late fall before cutting stems to the ground.

CULTIVARS AND RELATED SPECIES: 'White Cloud'—Larger foliage and flowers than the species, up to 7" to 9" across.
'Ray Hartman'—Finely divided leaves and 4" to 5" diameter flowers. More manageable for smaller spaces.

CALIFORNIA

Salvia apiana

WHITE SAGE

NATIVE HABITAT: Coastal sage scrub plant communities below 3,000' from Baja California to northern California and, periodically, chaparral and yellow-pine forests up to 5,000'.

HARDINESS ZONE: USDA 9-10, Sunset 7-24

OUTSTANDING FEATURES: A robust plant with distinctive chalky white foliage and bold flowering character, providing striking contrast to other garden plants. Tall, upright flower stalks reach 4' to 6' high, extending well above the foliage.

HABIT AND GARDEN USE: This fast-growing species has a dense and mounding habit when young, but opens and spreads after three to four years to 3' to 5' tall, and as wide. Lightly toothed, lance-shaped leaves grow 1' to 3' long on clusters of herbaceous and woody stems. Best suited to background areas in mixed perennial and shrub plantings, with penstemons, creeping sages, buckwheats and California poppies.

HOW TO GROW: Plant from containers in late fall in well-drained soil with little organic matter in full sun. Water every one to two weeks until onset of winter rains, and prune immediately after flowering to encourage dense foliage growth. Requires no summer water after first winter, but monthly drip irrigation will help retain good foliage character through late summer and fall. No pests or diseases.

CULTIVARS AND RELATED SPECIES: None.

CALIFORNIA BLUE-EYED GRASS

NATIVE HABITAT: Many plant communities throughout California and Oregon, most frequently in open grassy areas below 8,000'.

HARDINESS ZONE: USDA 9-10, Sunset 4-24

OUTSTANDING FEATURES: A miniature iris-type plant with handsome texture and intensely colored flowers. Develops a tight clumping habit and produces numerous clusters of tiny 1/2"-diameter dark purple-blue flowers with yellow centers.

HABIT AND GARDEN USE: This seasonal plant has upright strap-like leaves 12" to 15" tall forming clumps up to 15" to 18" in diameter. Deep green foliage develops from rhizomes in late winter and maintains good character until late summer drought stress brings on dormancy. Delightful with native bunchgrasses and annual flowers, and as an understory duff among large trees. Ideal for mass planting and naturalization in meadow landscapes and among spring wildflowers, where it can provide bold color in mid- to late spring.

HOW TO GROW: Best planted from container or divisions in late winter to early

spring. Prefers well-drained soils, sunny locations and consistent soil moisture to sustain its flowering cycle through late spring. Allow plants to dry and seeds to mature in late summer before removing spent foliage.

CULTIVARS AND RELATED SPECIES: 'Rocky Point'—Dwarf with extremely dense clumps, to 9" tall, 10" to 12" across, with broader leaves and larger flowers.

Other forms of *S. bellum* include those with white or uncommonly large flowers.

CALIFORNIA

SOURCES OF NATIVE PERENNIALS

A HIGH COUNTRY GARDEN
2902 Rufina St.
Santa Fe, NM 87505-2929
(505) 473-2700

AMANDA'S GARDEN
8410 Harpers Ferry Rd.
Springwater, NY 14560
(716) 669-2275

ANDRE VIETTE FARM & NURSERY
Rte. 1, Box 16
Fishersville, VA 22939
(703) 943-2315

APALACHEE NURSERY
1333 Kinsey Dairy Rd.
Turtletown, TN 37391
(615) 496-7246

APPALACHIAN WILDFLOWER NURSERY
Rte. 1, Box 275A
Reedsville, PA 17084
(717) 667-6998

CARROLL NURSERIES
P.O. Box 310
Westminster, MD 21158
(410) 848-5422

CROWNSVILLE NURSERY
P.O. Box 797
Crownsville, MD 21032
(410) 849-3143

ECO-GARDENS
P.O. Box 1227
Decatur, GA 30031
(404) 294-6468

EASTERN PLANT SPECIALTIES
Box 226
Georgetown, ME 04548
(207) 371-2888

FORESTFARM
990 Tetherow Rd.
Williams, OR 97544-9599
(503) 846-7269

LAFAYETTE HOME NURSERY
1 Nursery Lane
LaFayette, IL 61449
(309) 995-3311

LAMTREE FARM
Rte. 1, Box 162
Warrensville, NC 28693
(910) 385-6144

LANDSCAPE ALTERNATIVES
1705 St. Albans St.
Roseville, MN 55113-6554
(612) 488-3142

LARNER SEEDS
P.O. Box 407
235 Fern Rd.
Bolinas, CA 94924
(415) 868-9407

McCLURE & ZIMMERMAN
108 W. Winnebago, P.O. Box 368
Friesland, WI 53935
(414) 326-4220

MOON MOUNTAIN WILDFLOWERS
P.O. Box 725
Carpinteria, CA 93014-0725
(805) 684-2565

NATIVE GARDENS
5737 Fisher Lane
Greenback, TN 37742
(615) 856-3350

NICHE GARDENS
1111 Dawson Rd.
Chapel Hill, NC 27516
(919) 967-0078

PLANT DELIGHTS NURSERY
9241 Sauls Rd.
Raleigh, NC 27603
(919) 772-4794

PLANTS OF THE SOUTHWEST
Agua Fria, Rte. 6, Box 11A
Santa Fe, NM 87505
(505) 438-8888

PLANTS OF THE WILD
P.O. Box 866
Willard Field
Tekoa, WA 99033
(509) 284-2848

PRAIRIE NURSERY
P.O. Box 306
W5859 Dyke Ave.
Westfield, WI 53964
(608) 296-3679

PRAIRIE RIDGE NURSERY
9738 Overland Rd.
Mt. Horeb, WI 53572
(608) 437-5245

THE PRIMROSE PATH
RD 2, Box 110
Scottdale, PA 15683
(412) 887-6756

SISKIYOU RARE PLANT NURSERY
2825 Cummings Rd.
Medford, OR 97501
(503) 772-6846

SUNLIGHT GARDENS
174 Golden Lane
Andersonville, TN 37705
(615) 494-8237

SUNSHINE FARM & GARDENS
Rte. 5
Renick, WV 24966
(304) 497-3163

THE THEODORE PAYNE FOUNDATION
10459 Tuxford St.
Sun Valley, CA 91352
(818) 768-1802

VERMONT WILDFLOWER FARM
Rte. 7, P.O. Box 5
Charlotte, VT 05445
(802) 425-3500

WE-DU NURSERIES
Rte. 5, Box 724
Marion, NC 28752
(704) 738-8300

WILD EARTH NATIVE PLANT NURSERY
49 Mead Ave.
Freehold, NJ 07728
(908) 308-9777

WOODLANDERS INC.
1128 Colleton Ave.
Aiken, SC 29801
(803) 648-7522

YUCCA DO NURSERY
P.O. Box 655
Waller, TX 77484
(409) 826-6363

HARDINESS ZONES

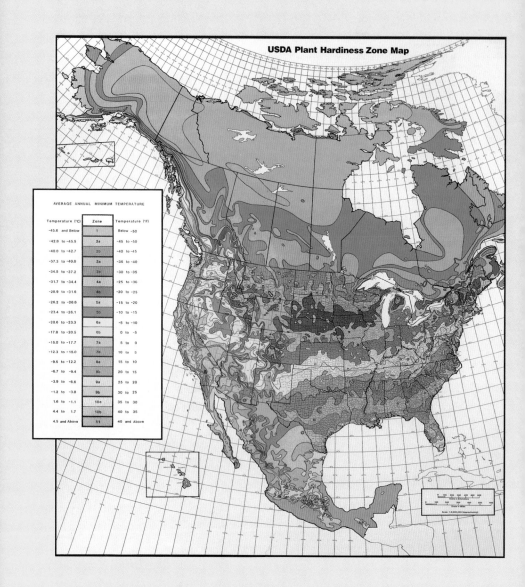

USDA Plant Hardiness Zone Map

AVERAGE ANNUAL MINIMUM TEMPERATURE		
Temperature (°C)	Zone	Temperature (°F)
-45.6 and Below	1	Below -50
-42.8 to -45.5	2a	-45 to -50
-40.0 to -42.7	2b	-40 to -45
-37.3 to -40.0	3a	-35 to -40
-34.5 to -37.2	3b	-30 to -35
-31.7 to -34.4	4a	-25 to -30
-28.9 to -31.6	4b	-20 to -25
-26.2 to -28.8	5a	-15 to -20
-23.4 to -26.1	5b	-10 to -15
-20.6 to -23.3	6a	-5 to -10
-17.8 to -20.5	6b	0 to -5
-15.0 to -17.7	7a	5 to 0
-12.3 to -15.0	7b	10 to 5
-9.5 to -12.2	8a	15 to 10
-6.7 to -9.4	8b	20 to 15
-3.9 to -6.6	9a	25 to 20
-1.2 to -3.8	9b	30 to 25
1.6 to -1.1	10a	35 to 30
4.4 to 1.7	10b	40 to 35
4.5 and Above	11	40 and Above

CONTRIBUTORS

NANCY BEAUBAIRE, guest editor of this handbook, is editor of *Country Living Gardener* magazine. She was a founding editor of *Fine Gardening* magazine and has contributed to several Taylor's gardening guides. She is a former owner of a landscape-design and -maintenance business in California, where she specialized in native and environmentally sound gardens.

C. COLSTON BURRELL is a garden designer, writer and photographer. He is president of Native Landscape Design and Restoration, Ltd. of Minneapolis, which specializes in ecological garden design.

RUTH ROGERS CLAUSEN is co-author of *Perennials for American Gardens* and writes and lectures extensively. She gardens in the suburbs of New York City.

KEN DRUSE is an award-winning photographer and the author of *The Natural Garden* and *The Natural Shade Garden,* and co-author of *The Natural Habitat Garden.* He lives in Brooklyn, New York.

JULIET ALSOP HUBBARD is a former curator of the New York Botanical Garden's Native Plant Garden. She owns Hubbard Nursery in East Taghkanic, New York, which specializes in North American plants.

KEN MOORE is assistant director of the North Carolina Botanical Garden, director of the Cullowhee Conference "Landscaping with Native Plants" and editor of *Growing and Propagating Wildflowers.*

BOB PERRY is a professor in the department of landscape architecture at California State Polytechnic University in Pomona, California, and principal in Perry & Associates, a landscape-architecture firm specializing in ecological design.

JUDITH PHILLIPS is a landscape designer and a partner in Bernardo Beach Native Plant Farm, which specializes in climate-adapted plants for residential landscaping. She has contributed to several Taylor's Guides.

SALLY ROTH, a lifelong naturalist and gardener, is a contributing editor of *Fine Gardening* magazine. She and her family live in New Harmony, Indiana, where they publish *A Letter from the Country,* a nature journal.

FELDER RUSHING, a frequent contributor to BBG's handbooks, is a seventh-generation Mississippi gardener and a horticulturist with the

Cooperative Extension Service. He is the garden columnist for the *Clarion Ledger* and author of the award-winning book, *Passalong Plants*.

GAYLE WEINSTEIN is owner of Eletes Consultants, a Denver firm that specializes in ecological landscape design. She also is consulting director of education at the Bernheim Arboretum and Research Forest in Kentucky.

ILLUSTRATION CREDITS

Drawings by **STEVE BUCHANAN**
Photos:
Cover and pages 13, 15 left and right, 16, 17, 19 by **KEN DRUSE**
Pages 1, 42, 48, 51, 52, 53 by **ROB GARDNER**
Page 5 by **ROSALIND CREASY**
Pages 6, 10 right, 23 right, 36, 39, 41, 55, 56, 59, 60, 63, 64, 65, 66, 84 by **C. COLSTON BURRELL**
Pages 9 left, 61, 71, 82, 85, 88, 96 by **CHARLES MANN**
Pages 9 right, 10 left, 11, 21 bottom right, 27 center by **RICK MARK**
Pages 21 top left and bottom left, 22, 23 left by **RUTH ROGERS CLAUSEN**
Pages 21 top right, 27 top and bottom, 32, 33, 54 by **PAMELA HARPER**
Pages 26 top right, 34, 35, 74, 75, 78 by **JERRY PAVIA**
Pages 26 bottom right, 43, 44, 57, 68, 70 by **JOANNE PAVIA**
Pages 30, 31, 37, 38, 40 by **JULIET A. HUBBARD**
Pages 45, 46, 47, 49, 50 by **KEN MOORE**
Page 58 by **CATHY WILKINSON BARASH**
Page 62 by **JIM LOCKLEAR**
Page 67 by **LAUREN SPRINGER**
Pages 69, 72, 73, 76, 77 by **GAYLE WEINSTEIN**
Pages 79, 80, 81, 83, 86, 87, 89 by **JUDITH PHILLIPS**
Pages 90, 91, 92, 93, 94, 95, 97, 98, 99, 100, 101 by **BOB PERRY**

INDEX

Gardening Books for the Next Century from the Brooklyn Botanic Garden

Don't miss any of the gardening books in Brooklyn Botanic Garden's 21st-Century Gardening Series! Published four times a year, these acclaimed books explore the frontiers of ecological gardening—offering practical, step-by-step tips on creating environmentally sensitive and beautiful gardens for the 1990s and the new century. Your subscription to BBG's 21st-Century Gardening Series is free with Brooklyn Botanic Garden membership.

To become a member, please call (718) 622-4433, ext. 265. Or photocopy this form, complete and return to: Membership Department, Brooklyn Botanic Garden, 1000 Washington Avenue, Brooklyn, NY 11225-1099.

SUBSCRIPTIONS

Your name ....

Address ....

City/State/Zip ....Phone ....

AMOUNT

☐ Yes, I want to subscribe to the 21st-Century Gardening Series (4 quarterly volumes) by becoming a member of the Brooklyn Botanic Garden:

☐ $35 (Subscriber) ☐ $125 (Signature Member)

☐ $50 (Partner) ☐ $300 (Benefactor) ....

☐ Enclosed is my tax-deductible contribution to the Brooklyn Botanic Garden. ....

TOTAL ....

Form of payment: ☐ Check enclosed ☐ Visa ☐ MasterCard

Credit card# ....Exp ....

Signature ....

FOR INFORMATION ON ORDERING ANY OF THE FOLLOWING BACK TITLES, PLEASE WRITE THE BROOKLYN BOTANIC GARDEN AT THE ABOVE ADDRESS OR CALL (718) 622-4433, EXT. 274.

American Cottage Gardening
Annuals: A Gardener's Guide
Bonsai: Special Techniques
Butterfly Gardens
Culinary Herbs
Easy-Care Roses
The Environmental Gardener
Ferns
Garden Photography
The Gardener's World of Bulbs
Gardening for Fragrance
Gardening in the Shade
Gardening with Wildflowers
  & Native Plants

Going Native: Biodiversity
  in Our Own Backyards
Greenhouses & Garden Rooms
Herbs & Cooking
Herbs & Their Ornamental Uses
Hollies: A Gardener's Guide
Indoor Bonsai
Japanese Gardens
Natural Insect Control
The Natural Lawn & Alternatives
A New Look at Houseplants
A New Look at Vegetables
Orchids for the Home
  & Greenhouse

Ornamental Grasses
Perennials: A Gardener's Guide
Pruning Techniques
Roses
Salad Gardens
Shrubs: The New Glamour Plants
Soils
The Town & City Gardener
Trees: A Gardener's Guide
Water Gardening
The Winter Garden
Woodland Gardens: Shade
  Gets Chic